The Four Intimacies

UNLOCKING THE LOVE YOU DESIRE

DR. AMY CLARK
ROY CLARK

The Four Intimacies: Unlocking the Love You Desire
Copyright 2022, Roy Clark and Amy Clark

All rights reserved. No part of this publication may be reproduced or transmitted in any form or by any means, mechanical or electronic, including photocopying and recording, or by any information storage and retrieval system, without permission in writing from author (except by a reviewer, who may quote brief passages and/or show brief video clips in a review).

ISBN:979-8-218-12884-5
Cover Design by: Nasrul
Interior Design by: Jose Pepito Jr.
Published by: Lovemaker Publishing

DEDICATION

This book is dedicated to those of you searching for an extraordinary intimacy that reaches the deepest parts of your mind, body, and soul. It exists, and you were born to be loved like this. We will teach you how to give and receive such a satisfying love.

Contents

Foreword vii
Preface ix
Introduction xi

Chapter 1   Relationships, Love, and Intimacy 1
Chapter 2   Intimacy Begins with You: Why We Struggle 13
Chapter 3   Verbal Intimacy 25
Chapter 4   Emotional Intimacy 45
Chapter 5   Physical Intimacy 73
Chapter 6   Spiritual Intimacy 99
Chapter 7   Keeping the Intimate Love Unlocked 123

Bibliography 139
About the Authors 143

Preface

This book is not a weapon to be used to point out flaws, failures, or the shortcomings you see in your spouse. If you purchased this book to guilt or shame someone who hasn't learned the language of intimacy or developed its skills, return it.

Instead, this book was written to promote love, connection, understanding, and intimacy. It must be read carefully and implemented patiently. You are worth the effort, though. You were created to be loved like this.

Introduction

As with all great couples, their morning started the evening before.

She had a long day with clients and wanted nothing more than to retreat to her sanctuary—her home oasis. While driving home, she fantasized about her husband and the hours they'd spend together before she returned to work the next day.

As she opened the door, the fragrant aroma of dinner reached her senses.

So much better than the fantasy! she smiled to herself.

She and her husband regularly took turns with just about every household task. When she spent a late night at work, he cooked dinner; when he worked late, it was her turn.

Placing her purse on the floor and shedding her jacket, she glimpsed a fresh bouquet of flowers centered on the dining room table, between dinner settings for two.

"There's my girl," her husband greeted her, with a long, tender kiss and hug. As he released his embrace, he turned and retrieved a glass of wine—offering it to his wife.

She knew that he had listened for the garage door to open before pouring the decanted wine. He had his routine down pat.

"I hope you're hungry," he said with a broad smile.

From the clients she talked with each day, she knew that eating meals together had become a rarity in most households. Family members often had different places to be to maintain their busy lives. Perhaps that's why she viewed dinnertime as a nearly sacred event.

INTRODUCTION

"Tonight, I have prepared for you..." he said, jokingly imitating their favorite show, *Chopped*, while serving her a plate of braised lamb, bacon and goat cheese laden brussels sprouts, and seasoned smashed potatoes. "And I'd love to hear about your day."

She thought of how blessed she felt that each evening, he'd ask about her day. And he truly listened to her response. Instead of trying to fix any problem or offer any advice, he nodded and asked more questions. If she was hurt that day, he was hurt; if she was happy, he was happy. With each story, he validated her feelings.

After dinner, they cleaned up the table and kitchen together before pouring another glass of wine and moving to the couch. Like most nights, nestled in his arms, she fell asleep entwined, while the television played in the background.

"Bedtime, sweetie," he said softly as he gently woke her and walked her to bed. On this night, he filled the water glasses to place on both nightstands. The next night, she would do the same—once again, taking turns.

Still slightly awake, she felt him crawl into bed and slide his arm under her pillow, wrapping his other arm over and around her. Their naked bodies fit together like puzzle pieces, as she backed into his embrace. She felt his sweet breath on her neck and the warmth of his leg, as he gently entangled his limbs with hers—his toes rubbing against the bottom of her feet.

They stayed locked this way for ten or fifteen minutes.

I feel so safe, so secure, she smiled as she began drifting off.

"Good night, my love," he whispered in her ear. Tonight, like most nights, he continued talking softly to her as she fell asleep. "You are so beautiful, smart, funny, kind, gentle, sensitive, and powerful. You are amazing in every way. Good night, my love, good night..."

Finally, they untangled their bodies and fell deep into a restful sleep.

The next morning, he rolled over and asked the same question he'd asked since they'd been together.

"Good morning, my love. Would you like a cup of coffee?"

"Yes, please," she responded sweetly.

INTRODUCTION

While he headed to the kitchen to make coffee, she freshened up in the bathroom. On her way back to bed, she lit a few candles. By the time he returned, she was sitting up in bed, surrounded by the glow of candlelight... waiting.

After handing her a cup of coffee, he entered the bathroom. She could hear him trimming his nails and washing his hands. She smiled. Within a few minutes, he crawled back into bed and cuddled close.

"How did you sleep?" he asked.

She answered and asked him the same question, adding, "Did you dream any dreams?"

While sipping coffee, they shared loving words in anticipation of their day. Once the coffee was finished, he took both cups and set them on the nightstand. Then he gave her a look that said he wished to explore her body in great detail.

Starting with her arms, he slowly began to kiss them. "I love your arms," he said with a warmth like he was seeing them for the first time.

Moving on from her arms, he explored her breasts, caressing them tenderly and covering them with his kisses, just long enough to send sparks throughout her frame.

Leaving her breast, his tongue traced her belly and explored her belly button playfully. Then he teased her hips and explored the soft flesh of her thighs. She arched her back in anticipation of what was to follow, letting out a long, slow breath as she yielded her body.

After what seemed an eternity to her, he finally explored her most vulnerable, tender areas.

Her back arched again as she pushed herself closer to his mouth, stroking his hair with her fingers. As she got close to the edge, he pulled back and explored her with his fingers, touching every line, caressing every curve.

"Like this?" he asked.

"Yes," she said at once. "Like that."

Like this? had become her favorite question. He knew exactly what he was doing and its effect on her. Still, he touched, asked, and received verification

INTRODUCTION

hundreds of times, always wanting to reach a new level of pleasure. Sometimes she answered with words; other times, she responded with soft moans to request he continue.

She couldn't take much more play. She was ready for what she really wanted—to be connected, to be one. Reaching over, she found him ready. *It's my turn to explore*, she thought to herself.

"Like this?" she asked him, taking turns as they savored one another's bodies with their hands. Through his responses, she'd learned when to stroke, stop, start, pause, and pick up the pace. She could read his every move and sound, but she wouldn't rely on his body language and nonverbal cues, even though she did that for a living.

While she kept him ready, his fingers continued to find her, pressing in and providing pleasure that exploded in waves.

This morning, she wanted to be on top. She felt powerful, strong, and in charge. Other mornings, she'd long to be devoured—to feel all his strength and security on top of her.

She thrusted herself against him as he pushed upwards to meet her. After such a long play session, they both were reaching their limits. They looked at each other in a way that communicated it was time.

They finished in a mutual explosion of moans and fast breaths, until they collapsed on the bed—still holding one another.

So much better than the fantasy.

"How does this keep getting better?" she asked rhetorically.

"I can't imagine any other way to start the day," he said as he tenderly kissed her face.

Instead of giving each other whatever energy and passion might remain at the end of each day, they'd savor each other in the morning—while awake, alert, and fully attentive to one another, before the distractions of the day took over. They made it their morning ritual; one they'd do nearly every day. Instead of scheduling time for one another on their calendars, they'd practice this passionately, without any sense of duty or obligation.

INTRODUCTION

When most people hear the word *intimacy,* they think sex. We didn't want to disappoint. Physical intimacy is critical in a healthy relationship. But lasting, fulfilling, and complete intimacy doesn't begin there. As amazing as it is to experience physical intimacy with your spouse, sex is not even the highest level of intimacy a couple can achieve.

And the story we shared is not fiction; in fact, it's a snapshot of how many couples live their lives. These relationships are the result of practicing the four intimacies in a specific order, each one unlocking the next.

And now, these intimacies and this process are yours to implement. In *The Four Intimacies,* we will spell out how you can achieve the pinnacle of human intimacy with your spouse, so what might read like fantasy today can grow into your reality.

The couple we wrote about in this story doesn't only practice verbal, emotional, and sexual intimacy. They incorporate spiritual intimacy in their relationship as well. Here's the rest of their morning….

An hour later, ready to start another workday, the couple sat in the kitchen—finishing their coffees and sharing satisfied smiles.

"What does your day hold?" she asked.

"I have a couple of meetings with clients, but I'll work from here most of the day," he responded. "How about your day?"

"Work will be a repeat of yesterday," she said with a joking pout. "And I'll take that every day, if I can have a repeat of last night and this morning!"

After a laugh, he held her hand and asked, "Shall we give thanks and listen?"

They spent the last couple of minutes in prayer together.

Are you ready for your story to resemble this one?

The Four Intimacies offers a research-backed tool to guide you and your spouse in building and living a relationship that would make a romance novelist blush. This book will teach you how to turn the most significant relationship of your life into the most gratifying experience you could ever imagine. We have researched, practiced, and presented parts of the Four Intimacies

INTRODUCTION

model to thousands of people, and now we've gathered our knowledge and experiences into this book.

Not all our learning came from books. We've learned some of it the hard way. We've both been divorced and experienced deep emptiness. We've made mistakes along the way and experienced the lessons that come from living both sides of the story.

After learning from our own failures—as well as learning from others during our combined decades of experience in counseling and coaching others—our desire is to help couples avoid living in empty, dismissive and especially abusive marriages, while serving as a potential blueprint for a healthy relationship and complete intimacy.

Intimate relationships require effort, attention and devotion. Don't expect to gain a phenomenal relationship without doing the work. But once you experience *true intimacy*, you'll never settle for anything less.

Our hope is to offer you a method and an understanding of how to *unlock the love you desire and experience each intimacy every day.*

~Roy and Amy Clark

We agree that sex is a critical part of intimacy, but sex is not where intimacy starts, nor is it where it ends.

Ch 1 Summary

CHAPTER 1

Relationships, Love, and Intimacy

What am I doing wrong? Marty asked himself in silent desperation. *What makes me so unlovable?*

Marty had dated several girls in college, and each relationship ended the same way: the girl eventually dumped him, leaving him alone. In the back of his mind, however, he told himself that few college dating relationships lasted. *Once I get out of school, I'll find a woman who's more willing to commit.*

But after nine years and three relationships lasting from a few months to a few years, Marty started doubting that he'd ever find a woman to spend his life with.

Yet Marty's parents managed to stay together for more than forty years. Granted, he wanted their longevity, but not their actual relationship. While growing up, Marty rarely saw signs that his parents truly loved each other. They seemed resolved, albeit grudgingly, to settle into the cold, passionless existence of roommates who paid bills together.

When his last girlfriend, Rachel, walked out on him, it seemed like she was reading from the same script his other girlfriends had written.

"I can't talk to you," she told him. "It's like we have nothing in common."

"We talk all the time!" Marty protested.

"We talk about nothing important," Rachel fired back. "We're basically roommates."

"Maybe you feel that way, but I can honestly say that I love everything about you," Marty started to plead. "I feel like we were meant to be together."

"You don't even know me!" Rachel shook her head. "What are my fears and dreams? What do I want to be doing in five years? Don't say that you know me... I'm just some girl that stayed too long."

"We have great sex," Marty interjected.

"No, *you* have great sex," she corrected him, "while *I* have empty sex. We don't make love. I feel like I could just as easily be a blow-up doll."

"You never complained," Marty answered defensively.

"And you never asked," Rachel fired back. "Look, it's okay. You don't get me, and that's alright. I don't think we're meant to be together. But I'd still love to stay friends."

Banished to the friend zone again, Marty thought bitterly.

It didn't take long for his anxiety to set in. Marty had experience being alone, but he had yet to find success being together with a spouse.

Then he remembered what his girlfriend before Rachel told him: "Maybe you should take a break from dating for a while. Just be single. You're good at that."

What the hell does that even mean? Marty wondered.

While eating take-out tacos alone that night, Marty let questions wash over him.

Why don't women get me? I'm smart, decent looking, and work a great job. Why can't any of them understand me? It's like they speak a different language. I shoot straight, tell them honestly what I'm looking for, and try to give them the same things I want in my life. Why don't they listen?

Marty wasn't alone in feeling like what he most desired seemed out of reach. This loneliness, insecurity, and dissatisfaction is all too common. Perhaps you, too, have felt that something is wrong with you, or that something is wrong with everyone else. You may long for intimacy, but find it like trying to catch the wind—it disappears the more you grasp.

It's time to demystify *intimacy*, so you can recognize, and capture, its replenishing power.

Let's be honest: we're not the first ones to write a book on intimacy. In fact, you can find hundreds, if not thousands, of books on the topic. Most focus on sexual intimacy, perhaps proving the words of the late actor, John Barrymore: "Sex: the thing that takes up the least amount of time and causes the most amount of trouble."

Sex is certainly a crucial component of meaningful intimacy, but *we believe that true intimacy occurs in the context of a relationship where two people love each other*. And that's why we are starting this book with a discussion of relationships, then love, then intimacy.

So, first things first: are you in a relationship? We know that might sound a little simple or obvious, but we've met with many people who are married, but they share little more than a street address.

Relationships are built from four essential elements. Lose one, and the relationship falls apart. And we're not just talking about a marriage relationship. These components are essential for *any* relationship—whether with a coworker, an employee, your child, or even God. You must possess these four elements to have a relationship with anybody.

> *Relationships are built from four essential elements*

The Four Elements of Every Solid Relationship

We use the metaphor of a three-legged stool to define a relationship. If you remove one leg from a stool, it falls over. If you remove the seat, the legs will fall apart.

3

Likewise, if you remove any one of the four essential elements of a relationship, your relationship will dismantle.

A solid relationship includes the following three "legs" of support:

1. **Time.** Time includes both *quantity* and *quality*.

   - *Quantity* means being physically present.
   - *Quality* means being emotionally present.

The act of merely "hanging around" together on the weekend or offering your remaining scraps of energy at the end of the day represents a lack of both quantity and quality. Taking a weeklong, luxurious vacation together is rich in quality, but doesn't make up for three months of neglect. A relationship requires both quantity and quality of time together to remain strong.

2. **Trust.** Building trust requires both *integrity* and *risk*.

   - *Integrity* means doing what you say you will do—being reliable with your words and actions. If you say you'll be back at 6:00, then be back at 6:00—not 6:30. This is a simple understanding, but a challenge to put into practice.
   - *Risk* is required in order to be vulnerable. By sharing your emotions, without knowing whether your secrets will remain safe, you're taking a risk. Trust requires keeping what was shared between the two of you.

3. **Communication.** Relationships must communicate to survive. The "silent treatment" and "ghosting" signal a relationship's demise. Getting frustrated when your spouse can't read your mind is another communication sign that your relationship may be on life-support. Active communication also means regularly sharing

THE FOUR INTIMACIES

your true thoughts and feelings, instead of saying what you believe your spouse wants to hear.

Communication has two components.

- The first is *speaking*—being able to share your thoughts and feelings through verbal communication.
- The second, *active listening*, is even more essential. Active listening involves confirming what you hear as you hear it. Asking good questions leads to great listening and a deeper understanding of the person speaking.

But the metaphor is not complete. A three-legged stool without a seat sounds like a primitive torture device. Keeping the stool together is the seat, which represents the fourth essential relationship component.

4. **Reciprocity.** You can give all of your time, trust, and communication to your spouse, but if your spouse doesn't return those in kind, your relationship is doomed to emptiness and resentment. A relationship requires two active participants who *give* and *receive*.

To take a quick snapshot of your relationship health, conduct the following exercise to evaluate the amount of time, trust, and communication you invest together—and how well it's reciprocated.

On a scale of 1–10 (1 being weak, 10 being "we got this"):

How would you rate your **Time?**
- How much quantity time do you spend together?
- Me ____   You ____
- How much quality time do you spend emotionally engaged with each other?
- Me ____   You ____

How would you rate your **Trust**?
- How well do you do what you say you'll do?
- Me ____   You ____
- How vulnerable and transparent are you?
- Me ____   You ____

How would you rate your **Communication**?
- Are you able to communicate your thoughts and feelings?
- Me ____   You ____
- Are you asking questions and listening?
- Me ____   You ____

How would you rate your **Reciprocity**?
- Are you meeting the needs and desires of your lover?
- Me ____   You ____
- Are you being filled with enough love to give?
- Me ____   You ____

Throughout our lives, we will have multiple relationships beyond those that we would call intimate. Think of the relationships you have with siblings, parents, bosses, coworkers, neighbors, friends, and extended family members. For those relationships to grow, you need time, trust, and communication.

This is even true within your spiritual relationship. If you want to know God or have a spiritual experience, you must spend time, take risks, and communicate with Him.

Hopefully by now you understand that intimacy requires a relationship. And true intimacy requires that your relationship is *loving*.

THE FOUR INTIMACIES

Word to Know: What Is *Love*?

The English language attaches the word *love* to a wide range of things:

- "I love this song!"
- "I love pizza!"
- "I love the view of the sunset from here!"
- "I love God!"
- "I love my dog!"

But when "I love" is paired with "you," those simple words take on a special meaning—one that transcends the physical and spiritual realms.

We define love as *a choice to direct your attention and affection towards another*. Keep in mind that since love is a choice, you don't actually "fall" in love in the same way you'd fall off a

> *Love is a choice to direct your affection and attention towards another.*

cliff. But with this definition, you can see that some people actually do love their pets more than their spouse—if they share more affection and attention with the cat… or pizza… or whatever else they love. Love is a choice, and for true intimacy to work between couples, each person must choose to direct their attention and affection towards the other.

Researchers from Rutgers led by Dr. Helen Fisher put what we call "falling in love" into three categories: lust, attraction, and attachment (Fisher 1998, 23-52). "Falling in love," also known as romantic love, happens when our brains are flooded with testosterone, estrogen, dopamine, norepinephrine, serotonin, oxytocin, and vasopressin. This type of romantic love is chemical and includes elements of those chemical explosions in the brain, especially around *lust* and *attraction*. However, a more comprehensive definition of love is *attachment*, which is the love that remains once those chemicals taper off and the newness of the relationship wears off.

Love is certainly full of feelings, but essentially it remains a choice. Directing your attention and affection to another is done intentionally, not accidentally or chemically.

People frequently use *making love* and *intimacy* interchangeably. And typically they're talking about sex.

We agree that sex is a critical part of intimacy, but sex is not where intimacy starts, nor is it where it ends. Join us as we redefine making love and intimacy, and allow you to experience both to their fullest potential.

Let's go back to the story of Marty. He, like many of our clients, never saw what a healthy relationship looked like. Instead, he stumbled along, trying to find an intense experience of oneness or closeness. He knew intrinsically that something was missing, but he remained unclear on what it was and how to get it. How could he possibly reciprocate with his time, trust, and communication, when all he'd seen were failed relationships? How could Marty dare to open up and begin the journey of intimacy without experiencing or observing such a relationship?

We wonder if Marty's definition of love described romantic love, instead of an abiding love—based on a choice to love *even once the chemicals stopped ruling his brain.*

So, what is intimacy? Our definition is very simple.

THE FOUR INTIMACIES

Word to Know: What Is *Intimacy*?

We define *intimacy* as *the intense experience of oneness or closeness with another.* The way you experience intimacy is based on two people's willingness to **yield** to another within an **exclusive relationship** that is **reciprocal**.

First, *intimacy requires yielding.* This is not a surrender, a giving up, or a giving in. Instead, it involves recognizing that you have something to offer, and being willing to share part of yourself with someone else. In yielding, we don't lose ourselves when we suspend our thoughts and feelings to pay full attention. When we yield our car, we retain all its power and control, as we choose to slow down and let others in. In intimacy, we, as Stephen Covey puts it, "Seek first to understand, then to be understood." In intimacy we put the other person first.

> *Intimacy is the intense experience of oneness or closeness with another*

Second, *intimacy requires some form of exclusivity.* Intimacy must include an element of privacy. It's impossible to have oneness with ten people. In sharing with so many people, we take intimate knowledge and make it common. Sharing information with everybody waters down and dissipates its sense of closeness and oneness.

Finally, *intimacy must involve reciprocity.* We cannot pour out without being poured into. If one person gives of their time, trust, and communication without receiving anything back, that person will soon be empty. Relationships and intimacy share the common trait of reciprocity. There is no room for martyrs within an intimate relationship.

In *The Four Intimacies*, we outline how to design the most critical and foundational elements of intimacy, which will support you while you grow as individuals and as a couple:

1. **Verbal and (nonverbal) intimacy** is a deep sense of oneness or closeness through communication. In verbal intimacy, we yield our voice, so we can hear the heart of the one who is speaking. Likewise, we control our expressions to show that we're fully present. What we share verbally is exclusive to a few. To experience verbal intimacy, *we ask questions and listen—with the intent to understand and a willingness to be influenced.*

2. **Emotional intimacy** is a deep sense of oneness or closeness through emotional connections. We yield our feelings so we can identify and empathize with the emotions of others. Once again, we share our emotions with an exclusive few. To experience emotional intimacy, we identify the other's emotions and empathize with them. While we might not completely experience the emotions or even agree logically with what the other person is saying, we do all we can to understand what they feel. At the time of sharing, the other's perception is their reality, and this is what we must embrace.

3. **Physical intimacy** is a deep sense of oneness or closeness through physical touch. We yield our desires to provide security and pleasure. Then we open ourselves completely to receive the same. We do this exclusively with one person. To experience physical intimacy, we see, touch, and feel one another with the intent of pleasuring the other person. By understanding our spouse verbally and emotionally, we provide security for them physically.

4. **Spiritual intimacy** is a deep sense of oneness or closeness through spiritual pursuit. We surrender our illusion of control, judgement, and understanding to experience a humble enlightenment. We are spiritually exclusive to a few. To experience spiritual intimacy, we must—together—earnestly seek One who is bigger than us, good, and mysterious.

Other authors covering the topic of intimacy include as many as twelve or more levels. We wholeheartedly agree that the concept of intimacy can be expanded to dozens of ideas and practices. In fact, we encourage you to include as many as you like. But if you wish to build intimacy, you must first incorporate these four intimacies as your foundation. Miss one, and you may still have a relationship, but not an intimate one.

Key Takeaways

- Relationships are built on the platform of *time, trust,* and *communication* and are sustained by *reciprocity*.
- Love is *a choice to direct our attention and affection towards another*.
- Intimacy is *the intense experience of oneness or closeness with another*.
- Intimacy requires *mutual yielding, exclusivity,* and *reciprocity*.

Before you can unlock the love you desire, you must keep in mind, that intimacy is not a singular act, but a series of progressive steps.

CHAPTER 2

Intimacy Begins with You: Why We Struggle

Chances are, as you learn about the roadblocks of intimacy in this chapter, you'll see how your beliefs and thought patterns impact your intimate behaviors. A healthy, loving relationship with yourself is a prerequisite to intimacy with another.

For healing to begin, you must:

- Know the voices that occupy your mind and shape what you believe about yourself and others.
- Know your emotions and learn how to express and control them.
- Know your body and what brings you security and pleasure.
- Know your God and how you relate to that higher power.

Understanding these four areas about yourself will shape and determine how you share and experience intimacy with others. What you believe determines everything.

Before you can unlock the love you desire, you must keep in mind, that intimacy is not a singular act, but a series of progressive steps—towards *verbal, emotional, physical,* and *spiritual* closeness, in that order. This is much like a combination lock. Not only do you need to enter the right numbers, but you must do so in the correct order. Intimacy begins with deep, meaningful conversations that lead to a strong emotional connection—empowering passionate touch, and then enabling an enlightened spiritual experience beyond yourself.

Many couples come to us confused. Some have a strong spiritual connection with God and one another, but they can't figure out why those strengths aren't fixing their sex lives. Or we hear from young couples who had great sex in the beginning of their courtship, but now they wonder if they really love one another. Others tell us that as a couple, the only emotional bond they share is in the love of their children. Notice that none of these examples began with sharing their hearts through verbal intimacy.

> *What you believe determines everything.*

Let's see how this plays out beyond your primary relationship. Have you ever said something profoundly vulnerable to a stranger? You may tell yourself; *I'm never going to see this person again. So why not?* And then you unload.

To your surprise, once you've unburdened yourself, the person embraces you with compassion and acceptance. Immediately, you feel like you've known this person your whole life. Odds are, when you revealed your most authentic self, the two of you connected emotionally.

Notice that the verbal intimacy led to the emotional intimacy. The more vulnerable the topic is, the deeper the emotional connection.

Let's go back to the couples who have told us that the only emotional connection they share is in their children. If they only talk about their kids, work, or the weather, it's not surprising that they don't share a strong emotional connection.

The same holds true in a relationship where only one spouse does all of the sharing of their heart and soul to a closed-off spouse. How can this lead to emotional intimacy?

What about a spouse who holds back secrets or parts of themselves out of a fear of rejection? That fear of being found out creates deep insecurity that you can never be known, understood, or loved fully.

The degree to which we share is the degree to which we can feel loved. If you hold back 40 percent of what you think or who you are, you can only feel 60 percent loved. Many couples come to us and say they don't feel loved, and we later find out they're each keeping their thoughts and emotions buried.

As we help couples communicate with one another, they experience a greater sense of love.

Why Does Intimacy Seem So Rare?

Look at your relationship with your significant other. You can gauge the health of your relationships by looking at *what you've become* because of your spouseship. Read the two following columns. Think about your spouse, and describe which column more accurately reflects your relationship.

Ask yourself, *Does my spouse (A)…or…(B)?*

A	B
Bring out the best in me	Bring out poor characteristics in me
Celebrate me as I am	Try to change me to suit their needs
Make me a priority	Give me scraps of their attention

You can be in a relationship, even if you have more items in the B column. But it's not a healthy one.

"Fitting in is about assessing a situation and becoming who you need to be to be accepted. Belonging, on the other hand, doesn't require us to change who we are; it requires us to *be who we are*." - Dr. Brené Brown

Positive, lasting relationships begin and strengthen because of the mutual joy that happens when two authentic beings can be themselves and feel loved.

You want more than a good *relationship*—one that is well-grounded on the three-legged stool of *time, trust,* and *communication* and shared in *reciprocity* between you and your spouse. You also want the kind of *love* that requires two people actively choosing to invest *attention* and *affection* into one another. But is that enough?

It's possible to have a relationship without having abiding love or intimacy. In fact, we know some people who are content to remain *unhappily* married—like Marty's parents, who we wrote about in chapter 1—just so they don't have to go through the work of getting divorced and starting over.

And it's also possible to have a relationship *with* abiding love—that is, love that persists—but without a full foundation of intimacy.

Intimacy is the crucial component that your relationship must be built upon, or your love won't sustain you when challenges arise. Nor will a relationship without intimacy enrich you.

Remember, we said intimacy is the foundation of your relationship. Intimacy allows you to build something durable, dynamic, and fulfilling—eventually adding "color" and "light" (your unique nuances) as finishing touches. Without intimacy, you'll never be able to enjoy the deeper rewards—akin to enjoying the finishing work of a home. Building a relationship with intimacy as its foundation is like making a house into a home, which may be why some in intimate relationships describe life with their spouse as being like "coming home."

From our research and years of conducting individual and couple's counseling and facilitating marriage workshops, we know the following truths about intimacy:

- It is very real and exists in every culture.
- It transcends every other human relationship.
- It can transform how we view ourselves and our spouses.
- It is available to couples willing to work for it.
- It continues to grow over time.
- It is rare.

Of all the truths we listed about intimacy, we're going to guess that the last one popped out at you. Before exploring the four intimacies, we want to explain why intimacy is so rare. The explanation is illuminating, but it also highlights some potential barriers you must overcome to experience intimacy.

THE FOUR INTIMACIES

Intimacy Barriers

From our counseling experience, some barriers surface more often than others. What follows is the short list of resistance points that our clients commonly share as intimacy blockers. You may see some common themes between them, or see yourself in these examples.

I Cannot Forgive

You've been hurt before. We get it. It's impossible to go through life without accumulating scars. And it's highly likely that your spouse has been the source of some of your hurt. After all, the more we know about another person, the more we learn about how to hurt them the most.

We'll spare you the psychobabble about *why we hurt the ones we love* and jump to the real issue: many people struggle to forgive those they love.

Regardless of how much another person hurts us, if we can't forgive them, we can't have intimacy with them. Unforgiveness is an intimacy killer.

Here's a secret: it might be time to forgive yourself.

I Allow Past Experiences to Unfairly Shape My Current Realities (and Actions)

Tied into our past hurt is how we often let past experiences—even from other relationships—influence our beliefs today.

Maybe you dated "Tony" for two years, and he broke your heart. You moved on and met "Jason," who couldn't be more different than Tony. But around the two-year mark, you start thinking about how Tony broke up with you. He didn't even offer you closure. Instead, he just said that he needed to move on. Then you start thinking, *Maybe I'll never have a lasting relationship.* Then you look over at Jason sleeping on the couch. *What if he does the same thing to me?* you wonder.

Whether you're conscious of it or not, you start pulling away from Jason. In response, Jason gives you space, which you translate into meaning that he's ready to dump you. As a result, you become irritable and argumentative whenever he's around.

Eventually, Jason confronts you about your actions, and you explode, "Why don't you just get out of here! I know that's what you're going to do anyway. So just do it now!"

And the cycle continues. By bringing in past baggage, you're dooming your current relationship.

You cannot have intimacy if you're unable to detach past hurts from the present.

I Cannot Release My Insecurities

Many people have a running tape of insecurities playing in their heads.

- *I wish I were thinner.*
- *If only I were better looking.*
- *I have a dead-end job. No one would want to be with me.*
- *My family is crazy. They'd drive off any decent person I brought home.*

Does this sound like someone you know? The truth is, we all have insecurities. Yet they are intimacy blockers. By thinking so poorly of ourselves, we project our insecurities and faults onto others. This clouds our view of others, and can even cloud their view of us.

The purpose of this book is not to address insecurities, but we can offer a few tips on overcoming them. If you affirm your own value, others are more likely to affirm your value, too. If you become comfortable with some of your left-of-center traits, people will be attracted to that as quirkiness. If you challenge your self-defeating self-talk, you will gain insight to see your many victories. If you treat yourself as important, others will see how special you are. If you make time to look for the good in your life, you will see good things all around you. In doing these things, you become a more positive, magnetic person—which will likely influence how your spouse sees you, too!

The bottom line is that until you overcome your insecurities, you are your own biggest barrier to intimacy.

I Have a Distorted Identity and Underlying Beliefs

American writer and family counselor Dorothy Law Nolte, PhD wrote a poem for a local newspaper in 1954 that she later expanded into the book, *Children Learn What They Live: Parenting to Inspire Values*. In case her name doesn't ring a bell, there's a chance you've come across the poem at some point. Her book sold more than three million copies and was translated into eighteen languages (Nolte 1972).

Here's a snippet of her famous poem:

> *If a child lives with criticism, she learns to condemn.*
> *If a child lives with hostility, he learns to fight.*
> *If a child lives with ridicule, she learns to be shy.*
> *If a child learns to feel shame, he learns to feel guilty.*

Not to point the finger at our parents, teachers, neighbors, clergy, or friends, but many adults carry identities and beliefs about themselves based on what others told them years earlier. And given the psychological phenomenon known as a *negativity bias*, we tend to forget the positive things others said about us, while long remembering the negative words they uttered.

If you still wear an invisible "L" on your forehead based on what others told you or said about you years before, you probably still carry that belief, even when your social groups and reality have changed.

Another example of distorted beliefs often occurs with those raised in strict Christian homes who grew up believing that *sex is dirty*. Either they were taught directly that sex is only sanctioned for procreation, or the topic of sex was so taboo that they assumed sex went hand in hand with shame.

We'll say more about this later, but you can't have healthy intimacy without physical intimacy. Period.

It's hard to find intimacy when we carry emotional wounds so deep that the words and actions spilling out of us communicate that we're damaged and flawed.

I Experienced Abuse

Tied into our identity and beliefs is also the too-frequent occurrence of abuse. Victims of abuse often look at the world through a skeptical and guarded lens. Those who have been abused may carry a diminished sense of self-worth and even lean into self-loathing and self-destructive behaviors.

If this is the case in your life, we're very sorry that someone (or multiple people) stole your innocence and view of the world as a safe place. In addition to offering you our deepest sympathy, we suggest that you seek a professional therapist. Talking to a professional can help you unwrap your abuse, allowing you to heal, love yourself, and see yourself as worthy of intimacy.

But sadly, victims of abuse experience a much tougher path to finding intimacy than those who haven't lived through such circumstances.

I Have Negative Motives

Some people enter relationships with unclear or poor motives. Have you ever found yourself in a rebound relationship? Maybe you wanted a quick distraction from hurt feelings over your previous relationship, but jumping into a new one too fast usually means you haven't taken enough time to figure out what you want. Some enter new relationships for revenge (as in, "I'll show my ex how hot I really am!"). Others stay in relationships because of low esteem, a sense of duty, social pressure, religious obligations, or a fear of being alone.

While it's common to operate with unclear or poor motives, it's not the way to start an intimate relationship.

THE FOUR INTIMACIES

I Have a Pornography Problem

Just because pornography is considered a social norm doesn't mean it's a healthy way to create intimacy. We know that this statement will make a few eyes roll, and some will wonder if we're suggesting that society move back to the 1820s. Just the same, pornography makes the list of intimacy barriers, because it comes up most often in our counseling sessions.

Here's how pornography blocks intimacy:

- Pornography skips directly to sex, bypassing other intimacies that must be firmly established first.
- Pornography dehumanizes physical intimacy, making masturbation, a blow-up doll, or a vibrator a substitute for your spouse.
- Pornography focuses on pleasure without effort or security.
- Pornography is about control; intimacy is about vulnerability and mutual relinquishment.
- Pornography can create increased insecurities about body image and sexual performance.

Pornography as a shortcut for sexual gratification is easy, and it's available 24/7. Intimacy, on the other hand, takes reciprocal effort. (We will share more about the problems with pornography in Chapter 5: Physical Intimacy.)

Our hope is that when you identify an intimacy barrier, you can dismantle it with the right support. The first step is acknowledging that some of what you've thought and believed isn't true, helpful, or positive in creating intimacy. You may require counseling to help rewire thoughts and let go of ideas that shortcut you from experiencing full intimacy. Without addressing these barriers, you may continue to struggle in your current and future attempts at intimacy.

If you have no potential intimacy obstacles, that's great! But it doesn't necessarily mean that you're living in an intimate relationship or experiencing intimacy in your relationship. We will explore this more....

Non-Intimacy Indicators

If you experience any of the following on a regular basis, these are likely signs that you're not experiencing a high level of intimacy in your life.

- Loneliness
- Resentment
- Temptation
- Addictions
- Jealousy
- Secrecy
- Feeling like a roommate
- No sexual intimacy or dissatisfying sexual intimacy
- Fantasizing about someone else
- Thinking about the person you "should have" married

In summary, we don't promise that achieving intimacy is easy. It requires you to let go of old patterns, baggage, and assumptions to embrace new, healthier ones. But one promise we can make is this: it's worth it.

In the next chapter, we'll start the intimacy-building process with the first cornerstone of its foundation: verbal intimacy.

Key Takeaways

- The four intimacies (verbal, emotional, physical, and spiritual) work in a specific order. Neglecting to build one intimacy, while skipping to another, often leads to an insufficient depth of overall intimacy

THE FOUR INTIMACIES

(like a combination lock that must have its numbers entered in order, or it won't release).
- Deep intimacy is rare and extraordinary.
- Achieving intimacy with another requires that we first work on ourselves.
- This book is not a substitute for therapy or counseling. If you have deep-rooted patterns from past traumas, please seek professional help.
- The simplest way to evaluate your current level of intimacy with your spouse is the presence of multiple non-intimacy indicators.

Homework

What barriers did you identify with in this chapter?
Do you have a healthy understanding of who you are and how valuable you are?
Are there any areas of yourself that you dislike?
Do you have anyone to forgive?
If so, who?
Do you have any triggers from past relationships?
If so, what are they?
What are your greatest fears when it comes to intimacy?
Do you have any past traumas that would stop or slow intimacy?
How many Non-Intimacy Indicators did you identify with?
Do you compare yourself or others to pornographic images?

*We ask questions and listen,
with the intent to understand and
a willingness to be influenced.*

Ch 3 Summary

CHAPTER 3

Verbal Intimacy

As humans in the current age, we communicate with countless people each day. Between texts, emails, phone calls, and face-to-face interaction, we spend about 70 percent of our waking hours communicating and interacting with others. We must be very good at it, right? Wrong! According to a recent study by the American Academy of Matrimonial Lawyers (AAML), communication problems were the number one reason for divorce in the United States. The study stated that about 67.5 percent of all marriage failed because of a breakdown of communication.

We also share certain information about ourselves with nearly everyone we meet. For example, we tell others where we went to school, what we studied, what we do for a living, how we spend our free time, and what we consider our favorite food. That information isn't private. It isn't intimate. These are superficial topics that we'd be willing to share with just about anyone. Consider it like the small talk you might make with your seatmate on a short airplane flight.

Verbal intimacy is different. Can you imagine a stranger sitting down next to you on your next flight, and you blurt out, "I'd love you to tell me about your biggest fear," or, "Who hurt you the most in your past, and how has that wound shaped the person you are today?" or, "Would you consider yourself traditional or freaky in bed?" Those questions might make the cut for a socially awkward character in a sitcom, but that's not how most people interact with people they aren't intimate with.

Honest communication is necessary for verbal intimacy. And verbal intimacy is critical to achieve all-encompassing intimacy with your spouse. So how do you get it?

> *We ask questions and listen, with the intent to understand and a willingness to be influenced.*

Words to Know: Verbal Intimacy

Verbal intimacy, as we define it, goes beyond talking or interacting. Verbal intimacy requires five unique characteristics:

1. It's *vulnerable*—showing transparency in sharing of ourselves.
2. It's *yielding*—silencing our voice so the other can speak.
3. It's *flexible*—demonstrating a willingness to be influenced.
4. It's *exclusive*—taking place only with those in our innermost circle.
5. It's *nonverbal*—including communication beyond just speech.

Verbal intimacy means *being vulnerable and transparent with another in sharing your thoughts, feelings, fears, mistakes, goals, plans, ideas, dreams, and passions.*

> *Verbal intimacy means yielding the floor and your voice to your spouse.*

Again, this is more than sharing your meal preferences. Saying, "I think I like dark chocolate more than milk chocolate," isn't quite the same level of vulnerability as saying, "I know I'm good at my job, but it doesn't fulfill me any longer."

Verbal intimacy means *yielding the floor and your voice to your spouse.*

Think of a strong, powerful horse. If a horse wanted to give a rider trouble, he could refuse his bit, buck, and throw his rider from the saddle. No man is as strong as a horse. But the horse chooses to yield. Similarly, verbal intimacy is built when each person in the relationship is willing to yield to the other in a cycle of active participation and reciprocity. In other words: shut your trap and let the other person speak without interruption.

Verbal intimacy means *listening, asking follow-up questions, and demonstrating your flexibility and willingness to understand and be influenced by what the other person says.*

This doesn't mean pretending to listen, while you secretly think about what you're going to say next. Too often, people listen just enough to argue or refute the other person's thoughts or feelings. Has someone ever asked you for your opinion, only to say after you've shared, "Okay, well, I'm still going to do what I planned to do"? To build intimacy, we listen to understand, not to plan our next verbal comeback. Then we ask follow-up questions to keep digging towards a greater understanding over what was being said and why. This shows that you value the thoughts and insights of your spouse, remaining open to learn from them or possibly change your views.

Verbal intimacy *is something that takes place exclusively with your innermost circle.* The proliferation of oversharing on social media indicates that many people are an open book to the world. But not everything should be shared with everyone. Your inner circle will include your spouse, of course, and perhaps your children, parents, therapist, and closest friend or sibling. But there's one topic that should only be discussed with your spouse, therapist, or doctor: sex. Nothing cheapens the intimacy of a physical relationship like complaining—or bragging—about your sex life with someone who's not part of the problem or the solution.

Finally, *nonverbal communication is, in some ways, more critical to verbal intimacy than the words we say.* Nonverbal communication comprises 70 percent of our communication. You must remain mindful of your body language and eye contact when your spouse is speaking; otherwise, what they *see* communicated in your actions will speak louder than anything you might *say*. Intimacy begins with engaged eyes, relaxed arms, and a forward-leaning body that says, "I'm here. You have my full attention, and I'm listening."

Based on the five essential factors (vulnerable, yielding, flexible, exclusive, and nonverbal), how would you rate your level of verbal intimacy with your spouse? Following is a ten-point rating scale. One (1) represents no verbal intimacy, and ten (10) represents so much verbal intimacy that the two of you could teach a class on the subject. Circle the number that you believe accurately corresponds with your current level of verbal intimacy.

1	2	3	4	5	6	7	8	9	10

If you rated yourself low on this scale, don't be discouraged. Many couples share a dissatisfaction with their verbal intimacy. Shortly, we will explore strategies to improve it.

For now, let's return to Marty. Remember Marty? His girlfriend, Rachel, gave him the "let's just be friends" line as she broke up with him. If you were to ask Marty, he would tell you that he thought that he and Rachel had great verbal intimacy. But they didn't. They exchanged words, but they rarely listened with a willingness to be influenced. They talked about "safe" topics, instead of vulnerable ones. See if Marty and Rachel's exchange next sounds familiar.

THE FOUR INTIMACIES

This Is NOT Verbal Intimacy

Rachel: "I hate my job."
Marty: "So quit."
Rachel: "And do what?"
Marty: "I don't know. But a ton of places are hiring."

Marty turns to pick up the pile of mail on the table.

Rachel: "It's just that when I studied graphic design, I thought I'd be creating art and using my education. Instead, I'm formatting newsletters that someone else wrote, and sending out marketing campaigns. A monkey could do my job."
Marty: (Flipping through the mail) "With all of the AI and automation, I'm surprised they haven't found a way to do your job with software. You basically do a bunch of cutting and pasting, right?"
Rachel: "It's reassuring to know that I could get downsized from a job I hate."
Marty: "It's just a matter of time before the only people working will be those who know how to build systems that can replace humans."
Rachel: "I hate my job."
Marty: "Uh-huh. Hey, here's a coupon for Chinese. Sound good?"

You can understand why producers aren't waging bidding wars over movie rights to the Marty and Rachel story. But let's look at Marty and Rachel's dialogue to see what they got right and where they missed the mark. First, Rachel made a bid for intimacy by sharing a sensitive thought: *I hate my job.* Good for her. But Marty? Suggesting that she *quit* is another way of saying, "I don't care. Do what you want." He didn't get it. His comment was dismissive. Tied into that, Marty didn't ask any questions to explore her thoughts further. Even after Rachel volunteered why she found herself frustrated, Marty essentially changed the subject to technology and how automation is the wave of the future. With his eyes on the mail and his body turned away, his nonverbal behaviors revealed that he found other things more engaging.

Rachel confiding in Marty about her feelings of career dissatisfaction could have been a relationship-building moment of building verbal intimacy. Given that Marty had already moved on to dinner plans, however, it became more likely that Rachel would find someone else to share her feelings with.

Ironically, many couples have conversations like this regularly. Some would even consider this scenario a victory, because they didn't end up fighting with one another.

Why Do We Get It Wrong?

Don't beat yourself up if Marty and Rachel's conversation sounds like how you and your spouse communicate. There are many reasons why we struggle to build verbal intimacy, but we'll focus on the most common one: *people haven't been taught how to*! And that often sets us up for misunderstandings from the get-go.

As we discussed in the last chapter, what we believe about ourselves and others can influence our emotions and behaviors. If Rachel believed that Marty knew how to give her intimacy, but withheld it from her out of choice, she'd feel rejected. This might lead her to behave—often unconsciously—in a way that ensures the relationship will fail.

THE FOUR INTIMACIES

How Rachel's Beliefs Could Weaken Her Relationship with Marty

Soaking in the tub later that same evening after telling Marty about her job frustrations, Rachel did some thinking.

Marty is such a jerk! I opened up to him about work, and he just says I should quit. Why is he always so insensitive? He just wants me to shut up. It's like he doesn't even care about me or what I'm going through, she told herself.

If those are the kind of thoughts Rachel embraced based on her beliefs and earlier conversation with Marty, how do you think she might act towards Marty in the future? Let's look at how her feelings and actions might change:

- She might stop sharing her feelings with Marty.
- As her resentment mounts, she might close off to Marty in other ways, like crossing her arms, not looking at him when he talks, rolling her eyes at him, speaking to him with a clipped voice tone, and having "headaches" at bedtime. Eventually, she might stop having *any* conversations with or feelings towards Marty.
- After she stops confiding in Marty, she might find someone else who really listens to her, like her coworker Roger.
- Roger seems to care about her.
- Rachel now finds herself with two potential romantic spouses moving forward: Marty the Insensitive, and Roger the Listener.

Which do you think Rachel will choose?

Roger that!

However, if Rachel understood that Marty was not a "jerk," but rather *ignorant* about how to build verbal intimacy, she might try having a different conversation with him. That doesn't take Marty off the hook for his part in the failed conversation. Rather, it shows how one person's shortcoming can trigger another person's insecurities, making the problem worse.

If you don't speak Hungarian, it's probably because you weren't born in Hungary and didn't speak Hungarian at home. Ignorance about one's communication missteps stems from a lack of exposure, not a lack of intelligence. In Marty's case, his lack of know-how about creating verbal intimacy comes from him not growing up in a home that modeled it, and from him not realizing that he had a skill deficit.

The good news is that Marty—and anyone else—can learn how to build verbal intimacy. If Marty could recognize that he had a blind spot in his communication and verbal intimacy, he would respond by saying, "I want to learn." Why? His longing for intimacy is matched only by his cluelessness about how to build it. So what's the solution? Read on....

What Verbal Intimacy Looks Like

Jack and Laura have been together nearly ten years. Today, they serve as a model for intimacy. But they didn't start that way. In fact, Jack shared in a counseling session that shortly after saying "I do," he wanted to reconsider.

The first few years of marriage required an adjustment for them both. Jack said that his father came out of the Military School of Manhood—"the strong, silent type"—where Jack learned to keep his thoughts and feelings to himself, preferring to listen silently instead of saying much of anything. The opposite was true of Laura's household, where her extroverted father would be the first to laugh, cry, and get everyone talking. Their different expectations and needs led to many nights where Laura would scream, "Do you even love me?" while Jack would think, *Will you ever stop talking?*

Fortunately, they recognized that they struggled with communication and verbal intimacy.

Jack and Laura: Masters of Verbal Intimacy

After a couple years of practice, Jack and Laura figured out how to develop verbal intimacy. Jack shared some of his thoughts about how he went from being the strong, silent type to the strong, compassionate, tender type in their relationship.

"I didn't know what Laura wanted from me at first," he explained. "Whenever she would tell me about any part of her day, either good or bad, I thought she was just talking to fill the silence. And when I didn't say anything back, she thought I wasn't listening or didn't care."

But Jack was listening, and he did care. That's why they entered counseling together.

"I finally figured out that what Laura needed from me was to show her that I gave a crap," Jack laughed. "That sounds bad, but that became my mantra. 'What would a person who gives a…I mean, *actually cares*, what would they say or do in this moment?' Before, I just did what my dad did: sat quietly. My father modeled sitting still and being talked *at*. So I couldn't look to him for that kind of advice. But I did some of the things I learned about in counseling to show her that I cared. Sometimes when she'd tell me about her day, I'd ask her questions to show her I was still tracking. When she shared something painful, I'd just say, 'That sounds rough.' And I started looking at her whenever she started talking. Then she talked less. It's like she kept talking before, because she wanted to be sure I heard her. By looking at her, she knew I was listening. And sometimes when she'd say something and I had no idea what *giving a…* looked like, I'd just get up and hug her. And that turned out to be the right answer."

Was Jack play acting? No. He addressed his wife's needs in a way she understood, while demonstrating his love and presence. It didn't always come naturally, but he learned to show verbal intimacy anyway.

Best Practices in Verbal Intimacy

In our research and experience counseling couples in improving their verbal intimacy, we've found that the strongest couples do the smallest things well. In this section, we'll explore some of those best practices of verbal intimacy.

Verbal Intimacy Starts with Asking and Listening

Verbal intimacy involves practicing communication and verbal "niceties" with your spouse. And that goes beyond asking polite questions like, "How was your day?" While that's a start, which can lead to verbal intimacy, you must truly listen to your spouse's response.

It's easy to be courteous to relative strangers like neighbors, coworkers, and acquaintances. You may greet them with friendly questions like, "How have you been?" or, "How are things?" This social etiquette we give to others is also something we must practice with our intimate spouse—as a start.

Indeed, asking "How was your day?" after you've been apart, if you don't already do so, is a simple first step to initiating verbal intimacy. But for that question to increase intimacy, it must be practiced with more depth than a casual question. It requires that you:

Listen to Understand. How many times have you asked, "How are you?" or "How was your day?" when you had no desire or intention to hear the answer? Sadly, this is a common practice. Listening to understand means you truly want to hear the answer and process what someone is going through. What is *their* perspective of the day and situation?

Listen to Empathize. Imagine your spouse responding to you asking, "How was your day?" by saying, "Today was tough. A coworker accused me of talking about her behind her back, which I've never done."

How you respond can range from *good* to *better* to *best*.

"I'm really sorry that happened," is a good response.

A better response is, "I'm really sorry. That must have hurt you. I know that I would have been hurt." This response shows empathy for your spouse's feelings, and it demonstrates that you at least somewhat understand what that must have felt like.

The best response is, "I'm really sorry. That must have hurt you. I know that I would have been hurt. Are you okay? Do you want to talk about it?" An offer to listen more in the moment shows care and compassion.

Listen without Judgment or Trying to "Fix." The American fitness company Planet Fitness owns a registered trademark on its brand: the Judgment Free Zone®. They offer a place for people to work out without the fear of being put down. Customers aren't expected to come through their doors with zero percent body fat or the physique of a conditioned athlete.

Likewise, the healthiest couples know how to listen without judgment. What is judgment in communication? Imagine your spouse telling you that she feels insecure, and you respond with, "Well, that's just stupid to feel that way!" That's judgment. The best couples refrain from judging the words and feelings expressed by their spouses.

And hearing isn't synonymous with fixing. An award-winning therapist friend of ours told us this:

> Most men like fixing things, and I'm no exception. Early in my marriage, my wife shared a problem with me involving a conflict at work. I thought I'd take on her situation to show

that I was a gifted therapist. She started telling me what happened to her at work, and after listening for a minute, I interrupted her with my solution: "Here's what you need to do…" Guess what? Wrong response! And I knew it was the wrong approach even as I kept talking! I would never treat a client that way, yet here I was telling my wife exactly how to handle her problem.

The next time she brought up a problem to me, she pre-taught me by saying I didn't need to do anything except listen. *I'll get it right this time*, I thought. God help me, this time I lasted two full minutes before I jumped in to tell her how to resolve the issue. The only reason we're still married is that I have such a forgiving wife.

> *Hearing is healing.*

Over time, I've learned that hearing is not the same as fixing. Hearing means suspending my mouth for as long as it takes for her to share her heart with me. Most of the time, she doesn't need me to "slay a dragon." She simply needs me to listen to her and validate her feelings. Hearing is healing.

Listen with Your Eyes. If you're like most people, you multitask to maximize your time. So it's not surprising that three out of four Americans admit to working or playing on their phones while on the toilet—which also explains why cellphones are ten times dirtier than toilet seats (Turner 2022).

But verbal intimacy isn't something to be raced or multitasked through so you can "check it off your list." In addition to plugging in with your ears, *verbal intimacy requires your eyes*. Think of an actor delivering the line, "I'm happy," along with an excited face. When what you hear and see align with each other, you have no problem understanding the meaning. Now envision an actor saying, "I'm happy," with a pained look. The same words were said, yet with a completely different set of nonverbals—and therefore a different meaning. Listening with our eyes allows us to both see and hear what our spouse is communicating.

THE FOUR INTIMACIES

Verbal Intimacy Deepens by Regularly Asking Vulnerable Questions

Verbal intimacy can grow naturally out of simple conversations like, "How was your day." But we deepen intimacy by initiating questions that leave us a little vulnerable. Here are a few sample questions to consider:

"Are We Okay?" This open-ended question opens the door for your spouse to discuss any concerns they may have with your relationship. This question is especially useful after you've engaged in what one or both spouses considered a challenging conversation or series of actions.

"Have I Disappointed (or Frustrated, Hurt, or Miscommunicated with) You Today?" In some relationships, this question would be like handing your spouse a loaded gun. But checking in to see if there's anything you can improve to escalate intimacy should be a regular occurrence. Asking this also removes any need for mind reading or possible misinterpretation of your spouse's behavior.

"Can I Share a 5 *Percent*?" In 95 percent of our verbal exchanges, we as spouses can easily discuss any topic in real time. But some topics—the hard ones to address—take planning to discuss in the right way and with the best approach. We use the words "5 percent" to inform the other that we want to bring up something that might be hard to say or hear. When a conversation is even more serious, we ask, "Can I share a 1 percent?"

Let's say that one of us feels jealous or insecure because of something the other said or did. Asking if it's a good time to discuss a 5 percent, puts both of us in the proper mindset. The proper mindset is one that involves listening with the intention to understand and willingness to being influenced, striving to remove any negative feelings that may have come between us. The wrong mindset—and the one that too often causes couples to argue—involves listening just long enough to deflect, defend, deny, or argue with the other person's feelings.

If you look at what most couples do when they need to have a 5 percent conversation, it's not hard to understand where things go off track.

At times, one spouse will bring up a tough conversation, only to have the other spouse swat it away: "You're the only one with the problem; I'm fine!"

Another common pitfall is that couples don't want to rock the boat, so they *avoid having tough conversations*. This can lead to resentment.

Another failure happens when one person feels wronged most of the time. In that case, 95 percent of what they want to discuss is what the other person did wrong. Yet constant nitpicking doesn't lead to intimacy.

The final common failure is being unwise when you choose to talk about a concern. The moment your spouse is rushing out the door for a meeting with an important client isn't a good time to have a heart-to-heart. Neither is it the right time when the kids are in the room, or at bedtime when you're winding down for sleep. These conversations involve important work, and they deserve your fully attentive time. Set a time, and be there for each other—to listen and learn.

When to Share a 5 Percent

Anything that continues to ruminate in your head merits discussion. Any concern that grows over time instead of shrinking should be talked about. Think of hurtful thoughts as fishing stories: they keep getting bigger every time you think about them. Here is when you should speak up:

- When your spouse says or does something that lowers your own self-esteem, makes you question your worth, induces guilt or shame, or otherwise destroys intimacy. Here are the kind of things we would consider worthy of a 5 percent discussion:
    - When your spouse cuts you off as a norm.
    - When your spouse says something that comes across as rude, belittling, unkind, or uncaring to you.
    - When you feel jealous and want to feel secure.
    - When you feel like you're carrying most of the responsibility by yourself.

THE FOUR INTIMACIES

But not every little irritating thing your spouse does needs to be discussed. Here are some of the most common (some are even comical) things that couples have conflict over:

- When your spouse puts the toilet paper on the "wrong" way, leaves the toilet seat up (or down), or doesn't put the cap back on the toothpaste.
- When your spouse falls asleep quickly at night while you're still wide awake.
- When your spouse loads the dishwasher "wrong."
- When your spouse leaves cupboard doors open.
- When your spouse folds the towels and sheets the "wrong" way.

These kinds of things aren't worthy of a big, formal discussion. They should be handled in normal conversation, like, "Hey, could you try to put the cap on the toothpaste? When I grabbed it this morning, I squeezed out half the tube accidentally." Many of the issues couples fight about—like which way to put on the roll of toilet paper—involve preference, not deeper values or a spouse trying to send intentional, passive-aggressive messages through annoying behavior.

Conflict arises when we tell ourselves, "If she really listened to me and loved me, she'd make the effort to put the toilet paper on the way I like it." Here's a thought: take five seconds to turn the toilet paper around, raise (or lower) the toilet seat, screw on the toothpaste cap, and tell yourself how lucky you are to have such a wonderful spouse in your life. If these are the biggest worries you're dealing with, count your blessings.

Verbal Intimacy Happens When It's a Priority

If we waited to go to the dentist, exercise, eat less, or have a colonoscopy until we *felt like it*, those things would never happen. What *does* happen in our lives is what we value, find worthwhile, and prioritize. Likewise, couples who find value in verbal intimacy are the ones who invest in it. They know that verbal intimacy pays dividends. And they safeguard the time they spend building it.

Couples who master verbal intimacy are those who schedule time to reconnect when stress is low, relaxation is high, and the phone is off. Along with the phone, make sure that your children are either in bed or old enough to know that this is your special time, where interruptions aren't allowed unless someone is bleeding!

Unless you schedule this time, it won't happen. If you don't prioritize this time, anything and everything else going on at home or in the world will seem more critical. And if you don't structure this time to hear one another, demonstrate your willingness to let the other person influence your own opinions and actions, and pour love into these moments, this time will feel punishing and will quickly die off.

Verbal Intimacy Homework

Start today by asking your spouse this simple question, a question you've likely asked hundreds if not thousands of times: "How was your day?"

But this time, keep the conversation going until this exchange becomes more intimate—the kind of discussion you only have with the one person you deeply love.

Listen deeply. If your spouse says, "Good," don't stop there. Ask, "What were some of the highlights?"

Instead of thinking about how you will answer that same question, keep the focus on your spouse. Follow up with questions like, "What would have made it even better?" Or if your spouse shares something difficult, follow up with an empathy inquiry like, "That must have been hard. That would have bugged me. What did you do?"

When the conversation is flipped, make sure you avoid one-word answers like "good or fine."

"Begin with the End in Mind"

In Stephen Covey's bestselling book *The Seven Habits of Highly Effective People*, his maxim for the second principle is, "Begin with the end in mind" (Covey 1989). This sage advice comes in handy for understanding the purpose of the simple question, "How was your day?"

"How was your day?" says, *I'm interested. I intend to understand you and know you. I want to know what you've been through, what you're experiencing today, and what you believe you will experience tomorrow.*

"How was your day?" says, *I value you so deeply that I want to know your thoughts and opinions. I esteem you so highly that I'm asking you to influence and shape me, even when it means changing my own behavior to meet your needs.*

"How was your day?" says, *I prioritize you. But when I ask you how your day was, I'm asking you alone, and I'm willing to hear whatever you tell me. That's because I belong to you exclusively. No one else holds my heart but you.*

If this exercise feels challenging, we'll assign it the way we did to Jack, in order to finally grasp what his wife wished from him. Answer this question: *How can you show your spouse that you really care?*

In the next chapter, we'll share the second part of the intimacy building process, as you create *emotional intimacy*. Not surprisingly, emotional intimacy is a natural offshoot of getting verbal intimacy right.

Key Takeaways

- While we spend a vast amount of our lives communicating, it doesn't mean we excel at it.
- Verbal intimacy requires vulnerability, yielding our voices to our spouse, a flexibility and willingness to be influenced, and exclusivity with our innermost circle. While verbal intimacy involves talking, it's also built through our nonverbal actions and what we *don't* say.
- The most common reason people struggle with verbal intimacy is that they don't know how to do it.
- Verbal intimacy begins with listening to understand, absorbing without judging or fixing, and tuning in with our eyes.
- Deeper levels of verbal intimacy grow less through what you *say* than by what you *ask*, such as: "Are we okay?", "Have I frustrated or neglected you today?", and "Can I share a 5 percent?"
- Verbal intimacy doesn't magically happen. If you want to build verbal intimacy, make it your priority.

We identify and empathize with the emotions of others.

Ch 4 Summary

CHAPTER 4

Emotional Intimacy

Before exploring the topic of emotional intimacy, we want to share some eye-opening statistics about extramarital affairs and the office. Did you know that:

- 85 percent of extramarital affairs begin at work?
- 73 percent of emotional affairs start at the office?
- 58 percent of employees surveyed in 2019 had slept with at least one coworker? (Cvetkovska et al. 2022)
- 22 percent of married couples in the US met at work, compared to 14 percent of engaged or married couples that met on a dating app? (Emery 2017)

At first glance, this data seems to indicate that the average workplace has more hormones raging through it than the Playboy mansion in its heyday!

But *what's really going on*?

People frequently spend more hours each week with a "work spouse" than with a life spouse. If you feel unfulfilled with the depth of intimacy in your relationship, you may look to have your needs met with someone at work, the gym, or next door, instead of your spouse.

Remember how we said the intimacies build off of one another, in succession? Verbal intimacy often directly leads to emotional intimacy. And emotional intimacy can quickly lead to physical intimacy. It's easy to see how investing in a coworker through verbal intimacy could progress that relationship to emotional intimacy, and so on.

> *We identify and empathize with the emotions of others.*

But here's the silver lining of that phenomenon: couples who invest in verbal intimacy can also easily turn that emptiness into emotional intimacy. And couples who experience emotional intimacy with one another form an unbreakable bond.

Let's make sure we are using the same definition of *emotional intimacy*.

Words to Know: Emotional Intimacy

Whereas verbal intimacy is about being heard, *emotional intimacy* involves being fully heard *and* seen, known, felt, validated, respected, trusted, accepted, made to feel safe, and loved by another. Emotional intimacy is that deep sense of oneness or closeness we experience through feeling connected with someone.

To create that "sense of oneness," two people must *feel* as one. Have you ever seen someone in obvious pain, their face twisted in agony? When you feel with that person, your face will subconsciously mirror their face, as if their pain is your own. It's called facial mimicry, and it's a sign of deep *empathy*.

Verbal intimacy asks questions and then listens, with an emphasis on listening. Emotional intimacy *identifies and recognizes the other's emotions, and empathizes with them*. The focus is on the other's emotions. We will define these actions in detail later in this chapter.

THE FOUR INTIMACIES

Emotional intimacy requires the same practice that Jack—our example in the previous chapter—showed his wife in verbal intimacy: *How do I show my spouse that I truly care?* And you don't need to be a linguist or an ophthalmologist to both *hear* and *see* the difference between someone saying, "I care about you," versus showing, "I care about you."

Emotional intimacy can be both *seen* and *felt*. Think of your favorite romantic comedy at the exact moment two people fall in love on screen. What do you see? What are their behaviors? How do you think they feel? How do you know that they feel that way? Now consider how you feel when you're fully heard, seen, known, felt, validated, respected, trusted, accepted, made to feel safe, and loved by another. That level of emotional intimacy is transcendent.

> *Emotional intimacy can be both seen and felt.*

Why do people "fall in love" at work, even when it can lead to the devastating consequences caused by an extramarital affair? Think for a minute about how you're likely to "show up" at work, versus how you "show up" at home. Be honest with yourself when you look at the following table. Where does the best version of yourself show up most often?

How We Show Up	Work	Home
Dress	Pressed; fashionable; clean-shaven; made up; freshly showered; sweet-smelling	Pajamas, sweats, and hole-filled clothes; prickly face or legs; *au natural* (but not in a sexy way); stinky
Energy	Friendly; charismatic; funny; sociable; likeable; warm	Worn out; grouchy; quiet; moody

How We Show Up	Work	Home
Focus	"Can do"; team-centered; ambitious	"Won't do"; self-centered; lazy
Attitude	Excited; "how can I serve you?"; willing	Lethargic; "here's how you can serve me…"; wanting
Manners	Please; thank you; excuse me; you're welcome	Burp; scratch; fart

In the office, we must work to earn the approval and acceptance of those around us. They don't *have to take us in*. Yet in "Death of a Hired Man," Robert Frost wrote, "Home is the place where, when you have to go there, they have to take you in" (Frost 1914). Do you reserve your best appearance, energy, focus, attitude, and manners for strangers and coworkers, instead of your life spouse? Or do you return home to your spouse spent—knowing that home is the place you *have to go*, for better or worse, because your spouse will *have to take you in*?

It's not hard to understand how the "work spouse" phenomenon can lead to infidelity. In an article called "Emotional Affairs At Work: Understanding The Limits For Close Office Relationships," the author offers this non-definitive list of warning signs that you might be falling into an emotional affair with a coworker:

- You talk with this coworker outside of work, after work hours, and/or about non-work issues.
- Your relationship with this coworker gives your spouse an uncomfortable feeling.
- Other people at work comment on how much time you spend with this coworker.
- You look forward to going to work, and you dread going home.
- You share things with this coworker that you haven't shared with your spouse.

- Your relationship with this coworker grows, while emotional distance grows between you and your spouse.
- You care more about the feelings of this coworker than you do your spouse. (Miller 2022)

We share these details about emotional affairs because the items on this list are examples of growing emotional intimacy—an intimacy that deepens relationships. We want you to think of and talk with your spouse throughout the day, every day. We want other people to be envious of your relationship. We want you to share your rawest self. That's a sign that you have emotional intimacy. And we want you to experience that deeply… *but with your spouse alone.*

Based on what we've shared up to this point, how would you rate the level of emotional intimacy you have with your spouse? Following is a ten-point rating scale. One (1) represents that you and your spouse have no emotional intimacy, and ten (10) represents that you have so much emotional intimacy that the two of you could teach a class on the subject. Circle the number that accurately corresponds with the current emotional intimacy level you have with your spouse.

1	2	3	4	5	6	7	8	9	10

If you're unhappy with your current level of emotional intimacy, don't be discouraged. This score—and, more importantly, your level of satisfaction with your spouse—can get better.

What if Marty Got It Right?

Let's go back to Marty and Rachel. If you recall, Rachel became vulnerable with Marty about her job dissatisfaction. For his part, Marty hardly listened. Instead, he offered cliches and a superficial, intellectual understanding of Rachel's dilemma. To top it off, he moved away from a moment that could have deepened intimacy, and instead he ordered Chinese takeout.

In the apartment across the hall from Marty and Rachel lives another young couple, Andrew and Beth. Andrew and Beth are newlyweds who have been married for eighteen months, but lately Beth has pulled away a bit as if she's distracted. Instead of waiting for the relationship to fall apart, Andrew takes off early from work to go grocery shopping and prepare a hot meal, which is waiting for Beth when she gets home from work.

Verbal Intimacy Done Right Creates Emotional Intimacy

Beth: "Why do I smell something good in here?"

Andrew: "Because I made something good in here for dinner. Would you like some wine or water with your meal?"

Beth: "Water, thanks. I don't understand. Did you get fired? Why are you home so early?"

Andrew: "Because I took off a couple of hours early to shop and make dinner for you?"

Beth: "Thanks… but why?"

Andrew: "Because I love you, and you've seemed stressed lately. Now we can sit down and eat without any fuss over what to eat. I also cleaned the pots and pans as I cooked. So, once we eat and pop our dishes in the dishwasher, we have the whole night to talk if you like.

Beth: "That's probably the nicest thing anyone's ever done for me."

Andrew: "That's sweet to hear. I just want you to know that I'm here for you."

Beth: "…I hate my job."

Andrew: "Whoa… That sounds serious. Is that what's been bothering you? Did something happen at work recently? Or do you mean you think you are meant to be doing something else?"

In this situation, Andrew isn't trying to *fix* Beth, because he doesn't see her as broken. He heard what she said, understanding that her feelings must be strong if she could utter those words. He then asks her to tell him more.

Beth: "Well, I don't know. I mean, I studied graphic design, because I thought I had some artistic skills. But I'm not doing anything remotely artistic. My degree doesn't even matter to them. I spend all day formatting newsletters that nobody reads and sending out marketing campaigns that nobody reads. I don't feel valued."

Unlike Marty, Andrew asked his wife a question that demonstrated that he not only heard her words but saw her heart. Beth became vulnerable by sharing, "I don't feel valued."

Andrew: "That must feel miserable. How long have you felt that way?"

With those simple words, "That must feel miserable," Andrew took verbal intimacy into emotional intimacy. Here's why: Andrew used *empathy*, not *sympathy*. Sympathy is when we relate to what another person says, because *we have shared a similar experience.* Had Andrew used sympathy by saying something like, "I've felt that way before at work, too," the topic would have shifted away from Beth and onto him. Andrew's follow-up question further demonstrated his desire to learn more about Beth's feelings. Had he replied to her feelings of not being valued with, "Don't feel that way," the conversation may have continued, but not in a positive way.

Because of the way Andrew heard Beth, Beth continues to share. Andrew yields the floor to her without passing judgment, interrupting, changing the subject, or offering cliches.

Finally, Beth has said everything that's on her heart, and concludes by saying, "I just don't know what I want to do next."

This is a crossroads moment. Andrew can hit an emotional grand slam, or he can strike out. Fortunately, Andrew is building verbal and emotional intimacy with Beth. He listened carefully and put himself in Beth's shoes. He thinks carefully before he offers a few thoughts.

Andrew: "I can only imagine how much that must frustrate and hurt you. But I just want to say that I know you have mad artistic skills. Look at your portfolio! Do you remember my mom's reaction when she looked through it? You're deeply talented, and I'm sorry you feel unvalued. I love you, Beth. Let's find a way for you to know how amazing you are."

Then Andrew hugs Beth closely, without sexualizing his touch or talking about dinner. He just pulls her close and sits with her in silence.

That's emotional intimacy. Andrew didn't treat Beth the way Marty treats Rachel. Instead, Andrew demonstrated emotional intimacy by doing what Beth needed most from him. He created an atmosphere for Beth to feel fully heard, seen, known, felt, validated, respected, trusted, accepted, safe, and loved. By directing his attention and affection towards her, he took their intimacy to the next level.

Why Do We Get It Wrong?

We don't fail at building emotional intimacy because we're selfish. Most of the time, we simply don't know how to grow this kind of intimacy with a spouse. (Reading this book is a step towards filling any gaps in your know-how.)

Additionally, sometimes we get it wrong because of other factors. This section will share some of the most common emotional intimacy barriers we've seen.

You Have Emotional Intimacy with Someone Other Than Your Spouse

Think back to when you were a child asking your parents for a snack shortly before dinner. If your parents were anything like ours, they probably said, "I don't want you to spoil your dinner." If you get your emotional needs met from someone other than your spouse, you're giving away one of the most sacred parts of yourself and ruining your appetite for a connection with your spouse. An emotional affair can "spoil" you from developing emotional intimacy with your spouse.

You Lack Depth in Your Verbal Intimacy

Emotional intimacy doesn't work like the Vulcan mind-meld on *Star Trek*. We can't read into the deepest thoughts of another through touch or mindreading. *Remember: the conduit for emotional connection is verbal intimacy.* Unless you have deep verbal intimacy, you won't ever develop deep emotional intimacy.

You Don't Fully Trust Your Spouse

We've counseled countless couples who worried what might happen if their spouses knew their deepest, darkest secrets. Might those secrets become weaponized against them during an argument? For example, if her spouse knew she had abandonment issues, might he threaten to leave each time they argued? Unless you trust your spouse completely, you won't experience deep emotional intimacy.

You Fear That Your Spouse Will Want You to Change

"She's going to want to change me," one man said recently in counseling. But guess what? Your spouse likely doesn't want to change you. What your spouse *does* want is to be heard, seen, known, felt, respected, validated, trusted, accepted, made to feel safe, and loved.

You Want Your Spouse to Agree with You

What would happen if your spouse loved all the things you love: food, music, television shows, fashion, vacation spots, hobbies, political ideologies, religion, philosophies, etc.? Your life would be more boring, and you would miss out on opportunities to learn, stretch yourself, and grow. Instead of insisting that your spouse "take your side" or agree with you when you disagree, strive to understand first and then be understood by your spouse. Verbal intimacy is about *yielding your voice, not sacrificing your identity, values, or beliefs*. The same holds true with emotional intimacy. The couples with the greatest intimacy are willing to understand and be understood, instead of insisting on being right or winning an argument.

You Shut Down, Choosing to Take the Path of Least Resistance

Deep conversations can be hard, and who would want to enter one if it leads to a fight? Maybe in the past you learned that confrontation only causes more problems. But this isn't usually the reality in relationships. Ignoring problems is often the best approach when the issues take nothing more than flipping around the toilet paper roll so that it's the "right" way or putting the cap back on the toothpaste. But when you feel *emotionally wounded* by your spouse, doing nothing isn't the answer. Our emotions work like resilient plants. When you bury them, they will resurface, often getting bigger the next time they show their tendrils.

THE FOUR INTIMACIES

What Emotional Intimacy Looks Like

Picture a first date where you instantly feel a spark or chemistry. Let's say the person across the table from you represents your ideal for physical beauty, whatever that means for you: eyes, lips, nose, hair, body with bulges in all the right places. This might not be love at first sight, but it could certainly be *lust* at first sight.

But then your date opens their mouth—which, by the way, reveals perfect teeth....

"I'm sure you want to know all about me," your date starts. And then, for the next sixty minutes, they talk all about themselves. Your date asks you no questions. Between their long, continuous monologues, looking around the room, and checking their phone, you wonder if you're on a hidden-camera prank show.

Emotional intimacy looks like the opposite. You have emotional intimacy when your spouse looks at you like you're the only person in the world. *You experience it when your spouse hears your words, senses your feelings, and seems hungry to know more.* Emotional intimacy grows when you feel safe enough to share anything—when you sense that the more you're known, the more you'll be loved. Emotional intimacy leans into you when you're vulnerable and reaches out to you when you're scared. When you have emotional intimacy with another person, you read their body language as if it's your native tongue, and you almost intuitively know what that person needs.

Best Practices in Emotional Intimacy

In our interviews with hundreds of couples on emotional intimacy, we have found that the best couples do things differently from the rest. The best spouse is one who engages in the following practices.

Give 100 Percent Emotionally at Home

Is anyone else tired after a long day, or is it just us? Fatigue is the norm after spending a day fighting fires, solving problems, finding consensus within work teams, and getting things done. And, yes, work can be emotionally draining. It's only natural that we want to come home, undress on the way to the bedroom, pop open a cold beverage, turn on the television, and decompress. But checking out after-hours with your most significant relationship won't develop emotional intimacy.

Imagine, instead of returning home with a mindset that says, "I'm done," you race home to pour yourself into your spouse. That's exactly what the best couples do for one another. They don't do it because it's easy, convenient, or their first instinct. They do it because the only way to grow emotional intimacy—a connection that is unique from the dozens of other relationships in their lives—is to invest like it matters. Because it does.

Take Time to Study the Emotions of Your Spouse

Unless your spouse is a professional poker player, you can likely tell a great deal about how their day went and how they're feeling by looking at them. Mindreading isn't required. But it's necessary that you look, ask, and make space for your spouse's emotions whenever they are evident. Put simply, emotional intimacy is fed when we focus on the other person's emotions.

THE FOUR INTIMACIES

Why We Cringe When Our Spouse Asks, "Can I Talk to You?"

Many couples fall into an unintentional trap when it comes to acknowledging the emotions of their spouses. Here's the trap: the only emotions that get discussed are negative ones like anger, frustration, disappointment, regret, and shame. Ask yourself if the following sound familiar:

- "I had the worst day ever."
- "I'm so mad about (insert complaint here)."
- "The kids have been driving me crazy."
- "I feel fat."

To be clear, we should be there for our spouse when they need to express their emotions. But those complaints can't be the limit of your emotional connection.

Instead, make room for positive emotional connections more often than for negative ones. Start by drawing out your spouse to help them share their positive emotions, or share your positive emotions with your spouse:

- "You look like the cat that swallowed the canary. Does that mean you had a great day? I want to hear about it!"
- "I just had the best drive home. Can I tell you about it?"
- "I had a huge win today! Can I tell you about it? (insert success here.)"
- "When I drove up, I saw that you trimmed the bushes that were growing over the walkway and even did some weeding. The yard looks great! I'm so lucky to have such a thoughtful

spouse. Thank you, sweetie. I love the way you partner with me to make our house a home."

Emotions are unique to humans and animals. Broccoli doesn't feel happy or sad when you choose cauliflower for dinner. But a dog wags its tail when it's happy and looks down when it feels bad for getting into the trash. If you love your dog, you enjoy how they communicate their emotions with you. Why shouldn't it be even more deeply satisfying when your human spouse chooses to express their emotions to you?

You can show your desire to create emotional safety for your spouse with a few simple questions:

- "Is everything alright? Are you okay?"
- "Are *we* okay?"
- "Did something happen?"
- "You seem (name the emotion you believe you see, either positive or negative). Penny for your thoughts?"
- "What was the highlight of your day?"
- "What's on your mind? And what else?"

These tiny gestures say, "I noticed, and I care." As former U.S. President Theodore Roosevelt astutely observed, "Nobody cares how much you know, until they know how much you care." Simple check-ins go a long way in showing empathy and a desire to be there for your spouse.

Emotional Intimacy Leads to Non-Sexual Physical Touch

Sometimes listening and asking questions isn't enough for certain emotions, especially when your spouse is less verbally or emotionally expressive.

THE FOUR INTIMACIES

Fortunately, touch doesn't require language. A simple touch of the hand, or the caressing of her arm, or the scratching of the back of his neck are all forms of nonverbal emotional connection. A close, tight, long hug is often the best way to show empathy, validation, acceptance, and love. This kind of touch is also an excellent way to make the other person feel safe.

The Magic of a Twenty-Second Hug

When you think of the concept of "kiss and make up," know that science backs it up. Researchers found that twenty seconds is the minimum time required for a hug to trigger the release of oxytocin, the bonding hormone (Escalante 2021). Physical touch and closeness help heal emotional dings by flooding us with "feel good" chemicals. Feeling out of sorts? Ask for a good, long hug!

Care for Your Own Emotions

How does self-care promote emotional intimacy? If you're not a strong swimmer, going out to rescue a drowning man will claim two lives. You can't be the life-preserver for another person unless you're in a safe place yourself. Both spouses must do what they can to bolster their own emotional strength. One person cannot carry everything for both.

Caring for your own emotions means knowing your limits. It's okay to say, "I'm struggling myself right now, too. I don't have anything to offer except my love and arms for support." Or you can say, "I'm hurting with you in that." Remember, hearing doesn't always mean fixing.

Emotional Intimacy Homework

As you might expect, as we add components to building intimacy, the homework will require more effort.

The first assignment focuses on positive emotions, and for good reason. We all hold what psychologists call a *negativity bias*, which is the phenomenon of our brains recalling negative emotions and events with more clarity and depth than positive ones. Focusing on the positive, however, gives our brains something more recent to embrace (Cherry 2020).

Practice #1: Explore Your Spouse's Positive Emotions

Step 1: Listen and Look for Signs of Your Spouse Expressing Positive Emotion (Good Humor, Happiness, Lightness, Joy, Pride, Excitement, Etc.). Some obvious verbal cues are phrases like, "I had an amazing day," "Guess what happened to me today!", "Wow!", or even laughter. Some nonverbal signals are smiles with an open posture, a happy dance, or whatever you normally see when your spouse feels on top of the world.

Step 2: Say and Do Something to Share in That Emotion. Come up with your own words, but convey this clear message: "I see that you're happy, and I want to celebrate with you!" What you *do* is just as important as what you *say*. Don't multitask. You can finish putting away the groceries later. Your office is probably not on fire, and if it is, whoever's calling needs to phone the fire department, not you. *Give your spouse your complete attention.* Move close to your spouse, and explore their eyes as if you want to read every drop of emotion they're experiencing.

Step 3: Listen with Your Eyes and Heart. You don't need to memorize the words your spouse shares. Focus on processing the utterance of their heart. Watch their body and nonverbals for signs of their emotional state while you listen.

THE FOUR INTIMACIES

Empathy: The Real Meeting of the Minds

Researchers have discovered something interesting that happens when we completely plug in with empathy, listening to another person. When a person shares an emotional story, a magnetic resonance imaging (MRI) scan reveals places in the brain that flare up to register emotions. Recalling emotional events literally makes them show up in our brains! But that's not the most interesting part. When someone listens empathetically to a person sharing the story, their brain MRI responds in the same way as the person who is telling the emotional story.

Your brain reveals how much—or how little—you're emotionally plugged into a person who shares their emotions with you. Emotionally plugging into your spouse means that your cognitive (brain) and emotive (heart) get actively engaged (Prochazkova and Kret 2017, 99–114).

Step 4: Thank Your Spouse for Sharing with You. When your spouse shares an emotion with you, they've just given you a sacred gift. A trouble shared is a trouble divided; a joy shared is joy multiplied. Imagine that your spouse just won $10 million. Doesn't that mean that you've also just won $10 million? Be grateful that your spouse wants their joy to become your joy.

Example of Sharing Positive Emotions to Deepen Intimacy

Anna: "Unbelievable!"

Tim: "The look on your face says something great just happened. What's going on?"

Tim puts down his phone and joins his wife on the couch.

Anna: "Do you remember that software client I pitched last month? The one looking for a new enterprise resource planning consulting?"

Tim: "Isn't that the one you said would probably pick the cheapest consultant they could find?"

Anna: "Yeah. Well, I'm happy to say I was wrong. I just got an email from the chief information officer telling me that of all of the consultants they interviewed, I seemed to fit best with their culture and needs. They want another meeting with me next week to talk implementation details."

Tim: "That's fantastic! I'm so proud of you! I've always known you're a rock star, and it's great to hear the same thing from your next customer! Way to go, sweetie!"

Tim hugs his wife tightly while kissing the top of her head.

Tim: "You really are something, babe. I know how hard you worked to get to this place of success."

You can deepen your emotional connection with your spouse simply by sharing in their happiness and successes as if they were your own. Because they are.

Practice #2: Explore Your Spouse's Negative Emotions

Fortunately, the steps of exploring your spouse's negative emotions align with how you prime your spouse to share positive emotions. In this practice, look for your spouse's negative emotion coming from an external source (outside of your relationship).

Step 1: Listen and Look for Signs of Your Spouse Expressing a Negative Emotion (Eyes Closed Tightly, Furrowed Brow, Frown, Tears, Sadness, Slumped Shoulders, Etc.). Again, some phrases are easy to spot in conjunction with negative emotions: "I had a bad day," "I don't want to talk about it," or, "Just when I thought things couldn't get any worse." If you know your spouse, you know that any change in their "norm" could be a sign of bottled-up emotions.

Step 2: When You Hear or See Negative Emotion Emanating from Your Spouse, Practice Empathy. Remember that empathy is feeling for another person even when we cannot personally relate to their experience. Look at the first column in the table that follows. Before looking at the corresponding second column, imagine how you would feel if you were in your spouse's shoes.

Situation	How You Imagine They Feel
Job loss	Like a failure; hurt; angry; shocked; sad; worried; anxious; despairing
Fight with best friend	Hurt; rejected; grief-filled; confused; angry; annoyed
Sick parent	Worried; stressed; sad; guilty; unprepared; exhausted
Low self-esteem	Despised; anxious; worried; unattractive; unintelligent; undesirable

When your spouse experiences a negative emotion, it's "all about them." Let it be. Offer empathy, give them an opener to continue—saying something like, "That sounds awful. I'm here if you want to talk through it."—and then yield your voice along with your emotions.

Remember that empathy is demonstrated in both words and actions, so make sure your actions show that you want to listen. Stop what you're doing. Look at your spouse. Don't rush or push them if they aren't ready to open up. It might take time for them to process their own emotions, and building emotional intimacy isn't a race. Sit near your spouse. Lean in. Touch them on the shoulder or knee. Let them know you're there for them, and then physically be there for them unless they ask for space.

Step 3: Talk Less, Listen More. Keep in mind that your role is not to *fix* your spouse or your spouse's situation. Your job is to fully hear *and* see your spouse so that they feel known, validated, trusted, respected, accepted, safe, and loved by you. When you're talking, you aren't hearing. If you're "fixing," you're focused on the situation instead of your spouse's feelings. If you argue about how your spouse *should feel*, you aren't validating how they *do feel*. If your words or actions reflect judgment, you're saying that you aren't safe and can't be trusted.

What Is Psychological Safety?

The Center for Creative Leadership researches best practices in work performance. They define *psychological safety* within a work team as "a shared belief held by members of a team that others on the team will not embarrass, reject, or punish you for speaking up" (CCL 2022).

While this definition fits organizational effectiveness, the same principle holds true for creating psychological safety in our most intimate relationships. How can your spouse desire emotional intimacy with you if they feel embarrassed, rejected, or punished for sharing their deepest feelings?

Step 4: Be Mindful of What Your Body Says. When we smell a foul odor, we almost always pull away, crinkle our noses, and cover our mouths. This response is universal. Why? Because certain smells trigger a primitive survival. Caustic smells may be poisonous and deadly, so we've developed a strong physical response over time to prevent us from sucking in air that could kill us (Reuters 2008).

Now think about what your body does when you're annoyed or offended by someone. If you're like most people, you close off your body by physically turning and looking away. You might cross your arms. Some people roll their eyes and sigh heavily, or tension spikes in their facial muscles.

As part of his research, Dr. John Gottman conducted a study with newlyweds, then followed up with them six years later. Many of the couples remained together. Many divorced. The couples who stayed married were much better at one thing: what is known as the third level of the "Sound Relationship House." Couples who made it "turned towards each other instead of away." At the six-year follow-up, couples who stayed married, turned towards one another 86 percent of the time. Couples who divorced averaged only 33 percent of the time (Zach Brittle, LMHC).

How should you respond when your spouse is triggered by a negative emotion? With acceptance. Instead of pulling away, work on remaining calm even if the emotions turn hot. Remind yourself that your spouse's emotion isn't about you; it's simply reflecting how your spouse feels. Be supportive physically through nods. Use facial mimicry in response to your spouse's emotions to show you understand and feel for them.

Step 5: Thank Your Spouse for Sharing Even Difficult Details with You. Negative emotions go somewhere. We can stuff them deep inside, or we can let them out. And if you've ever tried to stuff your feelings, you know that leads to them later exploding outward. Be the one person your spouse trusts to share their troubles with. Remember: "a trouble shared is a trouble divided."

Some of you have found the homework assignments easy. If that's the case, good for you! Keep doing what you're doing. But this was new to some of you. And you struggled, likely with the exercise about hearing negative emotions. Don't give up. Contrary to what we've all been told, *practice does not make perfect*. Practice makes permanent. Only *perfect practice makes perfect.* Reread the steps and try to do one thing better next time. If the steps feel too prescribed, go back to the simple ah-ha moment that Jack had about how to show up for his wife: *treat your spouse like you actually care.* That leads to greater emotional intimacy.

Deeper Practice

For Deeper Practice—which is what we will call our content in this book that allows you to take your homework to another level—we want you to complete two additional exercises. The first is for you and your spouse to do together during a time of no emotional conflict. The second is one we'd like you to practice in "real-time" when one or both of you are under emotional strain. And here's the kicker: ensure that the conflict is between the two of you, instead of coming from an outside force.

Deeper Practice 1: Help Me Know How to Love You More Deeply

This exercise combines both verbal and emotional intimacy, and it's designed to reinforce the reciprocal nature of a relationship as well as to draw you and your spouse closer. Ask and answer each question with your spouse, taking turns as you go through them. For example, both of you will ask and answer question #1, and then move to question #2 until you're done.

Note: Have paper handy to record your thoughts and apply what you hear later. Also, some of these questions are difficult, meaning that you will be asking your spouse for feedback that is personal to their feelings about you. Don't allow this time to become defensive. Instead, arm yourself with these two responses that you can use as you listen to your spouse:

1. "Can you say something more about that?"
2. "Thanks for trusting me with that."

THE FOUR INTIMACIES

One final note is this: Have fun! This is your life partner, the one you plan to spend the rest of your life with. Grow and enjoy in the journey. *Note: These are just ideas.*

Question 1: "What do you enjoy most about me as your spouse?"
Question 2: "What do you consider your single greatest trait?"
Question 3: "What is your happiest memory of the two of us together?"
Question 4: "What do you consider as the greatest accomplishment in your life?"
Question 5: "When have you felt most proud of me?"
Question 6: "If you could have one do-over in your life, what would it be? Why?"
Question 7: "What would your perfect day with me look like? What would we do?"
Question 8: "What is something you wish I would stop doing or do less often?"
Question 9: "What is something you wish I would start doing or do more often?"
Question 10: "What are three things that I say or do that make you feel loved?"
Question 11: "Is there anything that you wish you could share with me but don't feel like you can? How can I make you feel safe enough to share it?"
Question 12: "If you could change one thing about yourself, what would it be?"
Question 13: "What is your greatest fear?"
Question 14: "Is there anything you can share with me that would help me to understand you more completely and deeply?"
Question 15: "Is there anything you've always wanted to ask me but haven't?"

At the end of this exercise, hug to give and receive oxytocin—and not just a quick hug. Hug for twenty seconds and time it. Twenty seconds is much longer than most people imagine!

Deeper Practice 2: Real-Time Emotional Intimacy

While the homework focused exclusively on eliciting and expressing positive and negative emotions triggered by external forces like work, friendships, etc., this exercise is to practice reducing friction within the relationship, like when you have a difference of opinion.

As we shared earlier, understanding someone doesn't mean agreeing with them. We're not asking you to sacrifice your beliefs, values, or identity to please your spouse, Rather, we're asking you to practice making your spouse feel heard, seen, known, felt, validated, trusted, accepted, safe, and loved *even when you disagree.*

Since this practice will come from real life, we won't attempt to create an artificial conflict for you, and you don't need to either. Conflicts will come on their own if you and your spouse are human. In preparation, look through the following scenarios as samples of how to destroy or build emotional intimacy when you find yourself in conflict with your spouse.

THE FOUR INTIMACIES

Sample	Destroying	Building
Your spouse must work late, meaning you must pick up the kids… again.	*Don't say:* "This always happens! I can't count on you. Why can't you say no?" *Don't Do:* Silent treatment; anger; talk under your breath; avoidance	*Say:* "Can I share a 5 percent with you? I'd like to talk through what happened today." *Do:* Breathe; identify your emotion; think about how you want to share it; keep the end in mind: getting closer, not further apart
His mom is critical of you, and he doesn't stand up for you.	*Don't say:* "When will you stop being a momma's boy? Choose between me and your mom!" *Don't Do:* Silent treatment; anger; slam doors; badmouth mother-in-law; avoidance; withhold sex	*Say:* "I need to tell you how I feel around your mother. I need to feel like you stand with me." *Do:* Sit together; take turns sharing your feelings; be curious about why certain things happen and don't happen, without judging
He spends money at a time you want to save more.	*Don't say:* "We'll never retire at this rate. You act like spending money is therapy." *Don't Do:* Cut up credit cards; lower credit card limits; hide the check book; take Venmo and PayPal off the spouse's phone	*Say:* "I'm worried we aren't saving enough for a nice retirement. It seems like you spend money when you feel upset." *Do:* Breathe; share your goal, a comfortable retirement, and then ask their goal; if you cannot agree on a budget, can you at least agree on being more respectful of one another's goals?

Keep the following principles in mind the next time you face a personal conflict with your spouse. Emotional intimacy happens when you:

- State your intention clearly up front, like, "I want us both to be able to share our feelings honestly, while maintaining respect and love for one another in the process."
- Hear your spouse's perspective instead of just airing your own.
- Take turns speaking without interruption.
- Offer empathy for your spouse and their emotions.
- Accept your spouse's point of view, even if you don't agree with it.
- Make your spouse feel safe in sharing their feelings.
- Love your spouse despite differences of opinions.
- Value the relationship more than you value being right.
- Apologize when you're wrong.
- "Kiss and make up" when you're done.

That's a lot to remember in one practice, right? Don't worry. In most relationships, you'll have multiple opportunities to practice!

Once you've gone through a real-world cycle, your work isn't done. Afterwards, we suggest a debrief where you sit and calmly talk through these questions:

- "What did we do well when we disagreed?"
- "What can we do better next time?"
- "Did I say or do anything that hurt you?" (If you did, apologize)
- "Do we still have anything left over that comes between us?"
- "Could I approach you in a better way next time?"

This debrief makes sure you're building ever-greater intimacy.

It's hard to have emotional intimacy when you ignore issues, back away from conflict when it flares up, blow up, blame the other person, or play the victim. Unless you talk through things, you'll never experience the transcendent sensation of being fully known and fully loved. Verbal intimacy is the vehicle that leads to emotional intimacy.

THE FOUR INTIMACIES

Key Takeaways

- To develop emotional intimacy, we must identify and empathize with the emotions of your spouse.
- Verbal intimacy leads to emotional intimacy.
- Emotional intimacy is that *deep sense of oneness or closeness we experience through feeling connected with another.*
- Emotional intimacy means being fully heard *and* seen, known, felt, validated, respected, trusted, accepted, made to feel safe, and loved by another.
- To develop emotional intimacy, we must prioritize emotional intimacy with our spouse above anyone else.
- Then we must strive for depth in our emotional intimacy by trusting our spouse, not assuming that our spouse will try to change you.
- Stop expecting our spouse to agree with you.
- Stop withdrawing when you feel emotionally challenged.
- Those who master emotional intimacy give 100 percent emotionally at home, take the time to study the emotions of their spouse, use emotional intimacy in conjunction with non-sexual touch, and take care of their own emotions instead of expecting a spouse to do it for them.

We yield our desires to provide security and pleasure.

CHAPTER 5

Physical Intimacy

And with the turning of the page, landing on our chapter about physical intimacy, men across the world raise their hands towards the heavens, saying, "Finally, we're getting to the good stuff!" while women simultaneously lower their heads and recall the apocryphal words of Queen Victoria: "Lie still, close your eyes, and think of England."

Stereotypes, like this one, are false. We'll share more myths and truths throughout this chapter. But first, we want to be clear about what physical intimacy *is not* as well as what it *is*.

Physical Intimacy Is NOT...	Physical Intimacy Is...
Just sexual intercourse	Physical touch including sex
Just reaching orgasm	A continuation of verbal and emotional intimacy that leads to a climax including orgasm
Fulfillment via multiple partners	Fulfillment via one spouse
A solo sport	A partnership
Me-centric	Spouse-centric
About numbers (length of an organ, number of partners, duration of activity, or times per week, etc.)	The depth of connection

A free-standing sexual act	An ongoing extension of love
Blending physical needs and body parts with another	Connecting verbal and emotion love with a physical expression
A means to an end	A means without end

This is also a good place to mention that this chapter is not a *how-to manual* on having sex, sexual relations, intercourse, copulation, procreation, getting busy, making it, hooking up, doing the nasty, bumping uglies, knocking boots, shaking the sheets, horizontal refreshments, getting laid, making whoopie, funny business, afternoon delight, jumping bones, getting lucky, tapping that, shagging, boinking, screwing, matrimonial polka, churning butter, or any other of the literally thousands of slangs and euphemisms for the physical part of intimacy.

> *We yield our desires to provide security and pleasure.*

Couples don't need a primer on the mechanics of aligning their genitals. Leave two adolescents with an attraction for each other alone on an island without TV, internet, books, or instruction, and they'd have no problem figuring out how to line up their body parts in a gratifying manner.

The challenge is with aligning verbal and emotional intimacy to maximize their sexual fulfillment. The struggle most couples experience is what comes before, during, and after sex so that it leads to greater overall intimacy.

Words to Know: Physical Intimacy

Physical intimacy involves becoming one with each other by providing security and pleasure through permission-based touch. You accomplish this when you:

- Create a safe place for your spouse to be vulnerable and fully exposed.

- Ask questions that lead to a better understanding of your spouse's physical desires.
- Communicate clearly about your own desires and reservations.
- Explore each other regularly.
- Prioritize the desires of your spouse above your own.
- Practice reciprocity.
- Practice physical intimacy exclusively with your spouse.
- Practice physical intimacy on a regular basis.

Based on that definition, how would you rate the level of physical intimacy you share with your spouse?

Following is a ten-point rating scale. One (1) represents that you don't even remember who was President the last time you had sex, and ten (10) represents that you have so much physical intimacy that you've had to put this book down twice since you've started reading this chapter. Circle the number that accurately corresponds with the current physical intimacy level you have with your spouse.

1	2	3	4	5	6	7	8	9	10

If you're unhappy with your current level of physical intimacy, don't be discouraged. It can get better. We'll show you how.

Physical Intimacy: Like an Oil Change?

Physical intimacy is not like getting an oil change every five thousand miles because you "have to, whether you want to or not." An oil change is a task, a chore. You schedule it when you have time, but it's not important enough to take a day off work to get it done. Instead, you try to fit it into your schedule when it aligns with other errands you "have to" check off your list, like grocery shopping, mailing a package, or taking your child to a play date. Aren't there a hundred other things you'd rather do then sit in a service station drinking burnt coffee while waiting for your car?

Interestingly, though, couples can strengthen their physical intimacy by examining a few ways that physical intimacy is similar to getting an oil change.

Both Require Communication

When you go to get an oil change, the person behind the counter talks with you, gathers information from you, and asks things like, "Have you had any problems?", "Do you have anything else you'd like me to take care of?", and "Do you want regular or synthetic oil?" They don't assume; they ask, listen, and then ask some more.

Many spouses don't get their sexual needs met, because they don't know how to share their desires or ask about the desires of their spouse. Instead of asking, one or both parties assume that doing "the act" is all that's expected and is, therefore, sufficient.

Both Involve Work to Earn the Other's Trust

Jiffy Lube doesn't just dive straight into your oil reserve! Even before they enter your vehicle to pull it into the service bay, they cover the driver's seat and floor to protect your car's interior. Then they do a physical inspection of your vehicle, top off your fluids, fill your tires, clean your windows, check your wipers, check your tire pressure, etc. An oil change is synonymous with a complete maintenance check of your vehicle. Anyone can change your oil. Jiffy Lube aims to satisfy you completely and keep you coming back.

Physical intimacy doesn't start by grabbing the "dipstick" and "checking the oil." It's about setting the mood and ensuring the safety, comfort, and satisfaction of your spouse. Physical intimacy isn't simply intercourse. It involves exploring parts of your spouse besides sexual organs, and providing security and delight in ways other than just penetration.

Car care experts tell us that moving parts cause friction. Over time, tiny metal shavings can enter the oil and grind wear into the moving parts that keep the engine running smoothly. Clean, fresh oil keeps the moving parts smooth, reduces friction, and extends the life of the engine.

Couples, too, experience friction, from sources ranging from a personal conflict with one another to work or family stress, fatigue, etc.

Practicing regular verbal, emotional, and physical intimacy reduces stress and increases relationship satisfaction. Research also shows that couples who enjoy regular physical intimacy are less likely to get divorced or see their relationship dissolve (Kinsey Institute 2022). Healthy couples make love often.

Cheesy oil change metaphor aside, sex is easy. But what happens before, during, and after turns mere sex into physical intimacy.

Do you remember Marty? Like many men, he has always thought of himself as a great lover. Rachel, ummmm, disagrees. See if you can relate to some of Marty's mistakes in the following example.

Six Ways Marty Hasn't Been a Good Lover

1. *Marty doesn't know how to flirt.* Instead of building up to the topic or finding creative ways to engage Rachel, he blurts out things like, "Do you want to mess around?"
2. *Marty views sex as something to fill a void.* He turns to Rachel and says, "Now that the commercial is on, we might as well…"
3. *Marty doesn't understand foreplay.* That's why he lasts as long as free porn clips—max, ten minutes.
4. *Marty invests only in his orgasm, not in the couple's intimacy.* Sexually, his actions communicate something akin to, "Want to race?"

5. *Marty doesn't put Rachel's needs first.* Often, after a couple of minutes, he rolls over and says, "That was good!"
6. *Marty doesn't build intimacy with his sexual actions.* Not surprisingly, he skips cuddling once he's "done." Sometimes he goes to sleep. Other times he gets up for a snack. Most of the time, he heads to the living room to play video games.

Ironically, most men think of themselves as great lovers. No man thinks he's a Marty.

Men, or whoever this applies to, highlight this next sentence in your book: DON'T BE A MARTY.

How Do We Get Physical Intimacy Wrong?

Couples often fail in physical intimacy for the same reasons they fail in verbal and emotional intimacy. They don't prioritize it or schedule time for it, so it doesn't happen. Or they let work, kids, the dog and/or life just get in the way.

What would it take to make love every day? It's not that we expect you to, but it does help you understand what is getting in the way of your physical intimacy. "Well, today we didn't because… and yesterday we didn't because… and this month we didn't… Asking the question, *What would it take to make love every day?*, helps us see and make physical intimacy a priority. Intimacy—not sex. However, if you could make love that included sex, if you could have all the intimacies every day; wouldn't that be incredible?

Physical intimacy brings some unique issues common to many couples. While this isn't a comprehensive list, it represents the most common challenges we hear in couples' therapy.

THE FOUR INTIMACIES

When There's "Another" Woman

We don't mean a real one, at least not in most cases. We're referring to pornography, which we've already touched on, but we now want to discuss it in the context of physical intimacy. We didn't place pornography at the top of this list of challenges because we're "old fashioned" or "moralistic." Rather, we see pornography as a clear barrier to creating physical intimacy. Consider these effects:

- Pornography sets up an unrealistic view of sexual relationships (Vedantam 2017).
- Pornography use makes it increasingly difficult to become sexually aroused by a human (Brower 2021).
- Pornography users lose interest in physical intimacy and may engage in fewer sexual encounters with their spouses.
- Someone who opposes their spouse's use of pornography may view it as infidelity and betrayal.
- Spouses often feel sexually inadequate when their spouse views pornography.
- Both pornography users and their spouses experience a decrease in relationship sexual satisfaction and emotional closeness.

Porn: What Is It Good For?

In *Archives of Sexual Behavior*, Nicole Prause, PhD, published a paper with the short, telling title: "Porn is for Masturbation." As Prause's title suggests, pornography (aka: visual, sexual stimuli) is designed to generate fast arousal and a quick orgasm from self-stimulation.

But this "quickie" comes at the cost of intimacy. Prause's research neatly summarizes the downside of viewing pornography on relationships: long-term spouses "suffer negative effects from [pornography] due to decreasing intimacy and poorer communication" (Prause 2019, 2271–77).

Porn doesn't ask you to shower, brush your teeth, put on deodorant, shave, trim your nails, or dress up. And porn would never expect you to cook dinner, engage in verbal or emotional intimacy, take a long walk on the beach, put your dirty clothes in the hamper, pay bills, or plan for retirement. Perhaps, that's why 40 million Americans regularly watch porn (Webroot.com 2022).

As if those aren't enough reasons, couples that view porn are twice as likely to get divorced than couples that do not. And divorce is clearly a barrier to physical intimacy (Vedantam 2017). As a friend confided in us about her marriage to a husband who used porn heavily: "I loved my husband, and I know he loved me and even my body. But when we had sex, it was as if he were having sex with someone else. He didn't seem to see me, but some image of what he wanted me to be, which left me feeling empty. And the frequency and availability of our sex could never match what he found online. This became a constant source of friction, especially when I gave birth to our second child and had other demands on my body." She also confided that his porn use didn't stop with virtual activity. Shortly after their baby was born, he progressed to an in-person affair, which ultimately ended their marriage. She added, "I always thought his porn use was relatively 'innocent,' but now I see how it led to an addictive pattern that eroded our intimacy and ultimately our marriage."

When We Carry False Beliefs

Many of the beliefs we embrace as adults came from our childhood via our parents, as well as through other major influences or events we've encountered.

Here are some of the beliefs people have told us in counseling, which can erode physical intimacy:

- "Sex is dirty."
- "As a woman, I shouldn't enjoy sex."
- "Sex is fine when it's to get pregnant and have children."
- "Sex is a wifely duty."
- "My wife is frigid."
- "It's not worth the effort."
- "He/she wants sex all the time."
- "We just don't need sex."

This book isn't a substitute for couples counseling or individual therapy, so we won't specifically address all of the previous comments. Instead, we'd like you to do these two things: First, look at how you rated your current satisfaction level with your shared physical intimacy. Is it where you want to be? Second, read over the previous statements, and answer for yourself if any of these false beliefs feed your own dissatisfaction.

It's possible that you're happy with your physical intimacy, even while holding onto false beliefs. In that case, ask your spouse if they're satisfied with the level of physical intimacy you share. And remember this: sexual dissatisfaction increases the risk of divorce and relationship dissolution. Intimacy doesn't happen when half of a spouseship is unhappy and unfulfilled. If one person has a problem, then you both do.

When We Have Differing Sex Drives

Men want it all the time, and women enjoy it about as much as a root canal, right? Wrong. Psychologist and certified sex therapist Stephanie Buehler, PsyD, found that low sexual desire is about equal between men and women (Andersen 2019). In other words, the tale of frigid wives and horny husbands is a myth. Most couples, however, do have one spouse with a higher sex drive than the other.

Just because someone wants it all the time, doesn't mean they *expect* it all the time. Desire does not equal expectation. And that's very important to understand. As a loving husband and wife, we love to make love, but that doesn't mean we expect it from each other all the time. We respect that there are other important elements to our spouse's life and to our relationship. It's when we regularly practice all the intimacies that we especially long for each other.

> *Desire does not equal expectation.*

What is the solution for mismatched libidos? Would it surprise you to learn that it involves verbal and emotional intimacy?

Do you remember the 5 percent rule we shared earlier? Sex can become a loaded topic, one that even the strongest couples struggle to broach. If you believe that your spouse doesn't desire you, your self-esteem suffers, which isn't an aphrodisiac. Feeling unattractive will make you desire physical intimacy less, not more.

Marriage and family therapist, Irene Schreiner, found that spouses with lower sex drives don't often have sex on their minds, so they don't "just 'get in the mood'" instantly. "[For] them to feel the desire to have sex they need to be aroused first. That's why regular flirting and physical affection is so important" (Andersen 2019). Does it make sense why we focus on verbal and emotional intimacy before physical intimacy? Unless you develop those prerequisite intimacies, you will likely remain less than satisfied with your level of physical intimacy.

When We Don't Talk about Sex

No topic is more loaded than sex. Sex makes us vulnerable. The only time we're fully exposed to another is at the doctor, on a slab at the mortuary, and when we're physically intimate with our spouse. Most of us don't prance around naked often enough to become comfortable sans clothing.

And physical intimacy involves more than just being undressed. It includes giving ourselves over to the desires of another, while allowing ourselves to enjoy one of the greatest pleasures we can experience this side of Paradise.

Imagine you're at a restaurant and get ignored for ten minutes. Then the server brings you the wrong drink and delivers your appetizer at the same time as your meal. Finally, you find a hair in your soup. What would you do? If you dislike confrontation, you might say nothing and suffer in misery. But you probably would never go back.

Now imagine you're at a great restaurant with friendly service, wonderful prices, and delicious food. But they forget to bring you a soup spoon with your soup. Wouldn't you say something like, "When you have a moment, can I get a spoon for my soup?" You can eat anywhere, but great places that get one, minor thing less than perfect are worth holding onto.

Now let's stop talking about food and make this clear point about physical intimacy: even great relationships aren't perfect. If you exited a relationship when you encountered your first problem, you would remain forever dissatisfied and never with any one person for long. Doesn't it make sense that instead of suffering in silence or giving up on your physical relationship, you talk with your spouse about how to improve your physical intimacy?

Let's look at what happens if you give up on achieving physical intimacy and avoid that part of your spouse. Here's what your spouse might think or say:

- *You aren't attracted to me.*
- *You're getting your needs met elsewhere.*
- *You're frigid.*
- *We have become roommates without benefits.*
- *Why are we even together?*
- *You don't love me anymore.*

Not talking about your physical intimacy is the surest way for one or both spouses to feel dissatisfied, unfulfilled, and unwanted.

When Sex Isn't Pleasurable

Stephanie Buehler, PsyD, found that 75 percent of women don't orgasm from "normal" penis-vagina intercourse. Most women need direct clitoral stimulation to orgasm. And 15 percent of women never have an orgasm (Andersen 2019). Yet men believe their spouse has reached climax at a much higher rate than they actually do (Lehmiller 2019). Research shows that most women need ten to twenty minutes of direct clitoral stimulation to climax (*Men's Journal* 2022).

Except for those with rare medical conditions, sex should never be painful and should be reciprocally rewarding for both spouses. If a woman doesn't find physical intimacy pleasurable, then the couple needs to communicate until they find a way to make it fulfilling for her.

When a woman doesn't enjoy sex, (and she has overcome her personal barriers) it's most often because her spouse didn't do his part to connect emotionally and then phycially satisfy her.

All Men Are Great Lovers, Right?

Men never claim to be perfect. In fact, many men we've counseled have been quick to admit that they aren't the best communicators and that they struggle to get in touch with their emotions. They find it easy to acknowledge that verbal and emotional intimacy doesn't come naturally to them.

"You could benefit from learning new communication skills," we'll say (as counselors).

"Guilty as charged," the man will respond. "You're right. I'm not very good at talking."

"Do you connect with your spouse's emotions when she shares something with you?" we'll ask.

THE FOUR INTIMACIES

"No," he'll admit. "Most of the time I think she's just talking in order to stop me from saying anything. I have no idea what's going on in that head of hers."

"Is it possible that your spouse doesn't enjoy physical intimacy because you focus on getting *your* needs met and not *hers*?" we'll ask.

Crickets. Shocked face. Squirming in his seat. One time an actual verbal response of, "I've never had any complaints," left us uncertain if we should laugh or cry.

Men universally evaluate their manhood by two factors: their prowess in bed and their ability to deadlift a refrigerator. But especially the bed one.

The mere suggestion that a man might not make his spouse scream (or whisper) in delight could sound like fighting words!

It's true that many men have more physical strength than the person they married. But men aren't any better at reading minds than women. That's okay, because we have the solution: if men don't develop verbal and emotional intimacy with their spouses, they'll never know what makes their spouse feel good, what they like, and what they'd like more of in times of physical intimacy. So, develop that intimacy!

When Physical Love Becomes a Weapon

Skipping physical intimacy until a mutually-agreed-upon time or for medical reasons can be a good thing for a relationship. However, withholding physical intimacy for other reasons isn't the way strong couples build and maintain a healthy relationship.

Some of the ways spouses weaponize love are subtle. Others are not. Here are some common ones we see:

Nagging and Criticism. Even men find it difficult to desire physical intimacy with a spouse who speaks criticism as a primary language. By tearing down verbal and emotional intimacy, physical desires diminish.

Letting Yourself Go. "I just don't feel sexy." Humans are visual creatures. Neglecting basic grooming sends a message to your spouse that you want to be left alone in the same way the barbs on a porcupine say, "Don't pet me." It also says to your spouse, "You're not worth the work." If you don't feel sexy, then do something about it. Get up off the couch and take a walk. Go to the gym and put down the bag of chips. And, no, a fruit smoothie in the morning is not a good idea to lose weight. You are worth it, and so is the one you love.

Being Overly Sexual in Public. The male peacock finds a mate by spreading its beautiful feathers and hanging them high. That's fine for a bird, and it's also something humans often do in dating to attract interest. But looking great for your spouse is different than seeking broad sexual attention from every person in the room. If you're intentionally, overtly sexual when you're out in public, you may be using your sexuality to gain power in your relationship, not intimacy.

Holding Sex Hostage. Most happy couples share chores and responsibilities around the house. The idea of a "honey do" list comes up frequently in counseling, and we're 100 percent in agreement that a healthy relationship is built on shared, reciprocal work and rewards. But it's unacceptable for a spouse to hold a list of items that must be done before being willing to have physical intimacy (Lyman 2012).

Physical Intimacy Is Good for What Ails You

Physical intimacy is critical for relationship health. In addition to creating happiness, physical intimacy offers a host of additional health benefits. Physical intimacy will or may:

- Improve your mood
- Boost heart health
- Boost immunity
- Reduce the risk of certain cancers
- Lower stress levels
- Improve hormone balance
- Lower blood pressure
- Improve women's bladder control
- Improve sleep
- Reduce the chances of a heart attack
- Lessen pain
- Boost cognition

This isn't a health book. It's a book designed to help you get the intimacy you've always craved. But the benefits are still proven: physical intimacy matters! In fact, committed couples that have regular physical intimacy experience greater overall intimacy and positive emotions in their relationship, even when the intimacy didn't include sexual intercourse. Clinical psychologist Anik Debrot led a study that reported, "Moments that [couples] experienced as erotic or sexually arousing [led to an increase in] positive emotions" (LaMotte 2018).

Best Practices in Physical Intimacy

Unlike sexual intercourse, which can be a one-time act, intimacy is an ongoing process that unfolds over time. It is tied to what we say, think, feel, and do. The foundational element of the intimacies lies on our willingness to be fully vulnerable, fully known, and fully loved. When two people commit to building a relationship around verbal and emotional intimacy, physical intimacy becomes a natural, healthy, bonding extension of love.

From the couples we've counseled and the research we've conducted through the years, we've found that the couples with the highest level of satisfaction in their physical intimacy do things differently than the rest—practices which we will share in this section.

Physical Intimacy Doesn't Need to Include Sexual Intercourse or Orgasm

Couples who cuddle on the couch, hold hands, and hug and kiss one another in nonsexual moments report greater overall intimacy. Physical contact like gentle touches, putting your arms around each other, and showing affection not only create long-lasting intimacy, but they also express that you love and desire your spouse.

If your spouse thinks the only time you talk, express emotions, or want to hold hands is a prelude to wanting sex, that's a sign that you need to regularly focus on talking, responding to emotions, and holding hands when sex isn't an option. This can happen when you're driving down the highway, sitting on an airplane, or attending a party.

Physical Intimacy Is Both Scheduled and Spontaneous

Sometimes it's nice to plan a long, relaxing vacation where you research your destination, choose the best accommodations, and take your time exploring and savoring every experience. Other times it's just nice to go for a short drive with your spouse.

The same is true with physical intimacy. Expect to plan some of your physical encounters. Doing so allows you to heighten your anticipation and prepare mentally, emotionally, physically, and sexually to take your time and savor every moment. But if you must plan every sexual activity so carefully, it can become work. As a result, you might not have sexual intimacy more than a few times a year! Regardless of when and how you get there, make sure it often happens at the best part of your day, rather than relegating it to the end when you're tired and worn out.

What a Great Time to Become OCD!

A client told us that her husband went to the bathroom right before they were going to make love. The next thing she heard was the sound of him clipping his nails. "What a great time to become OCD!" she thought. Talk about a mood killer!

But she thought differently when he came back into the bedroom and said, "Sorry, I just wanted to make sure my nails were trimmed, because I didn't want a sharp edge to hurt you."

The woman told us how that small act *and his communication about it* made her feel incredibly loved and safe. "He *really* cares about me," she said.

Because her husband used verbal intimacy to explain what he was doing and why, he added a layer of security and took her physical intimacy to a new level.

Balance your planned sexual activities with spontaneous ones. Nothing fuels passion like showing your spouse that you find them desirable. Having a quick sexual encounter with your spouse with no planning communicates, "You're always on my mind, and I can't help but want you."

In every case where we interview a couple with satisfying, fulfilling physical intimacy, they tell us that they make it a priority. If they're too tired to make love in the evening, they connect in the morning. If they have a hard time waking up in the morning, they carve out time at night.

Physical Intimacy Starts Between Your Ears

Therapists know that the most critical sex organ isn't between our legs, it's between our ears. Sexual activity is physical, chemical, emotional, and psychological—all things that start in the brain, not in any sex organ. Our brains send, receive, and translate sexual activity and it directly affect if we find something pleasurable or not (Surendra and Deshpande 2021).

Men generally require less to become sexually aroused than women. Explaining what women need to become sexually aroused, psychotherapist Esther Perel put it this way: "For women there is a need for a plot—hence the romance novel. It is more about the anticipation, how you get there; it is the longing that is the fuel for desire" (Sine 2013). A man who builds verbal and emotional intimacy with his spouse often unlocks her desire to crave physical intimacy.

Do You Want to Have Physical Intimacy with Your Spouse Today?

Behave towards your spouse today in a way that makes them feel close, playful, aligned, respected, valued, appreciated, safe, heard, and loved. Make sure you have no known unresolved issues or resentment between you.

Men, highlight this next part. *Remember, women need more time to become aroused. Negative emotions, insecurities, and poor verbal and emotional intimacy make it even more unlikely that your spouse will respond to physical overtures.*

Treating your spouse with such passionate care throughout the day becomes extended emotional foreplay, and will increase any physical response of gratitude.

For those in a committed relationship, consider sexting to stoke the fires even when your spouse is physically out of reach. We know that readers adhering to the most Christian, puritanical values might find this shocking, even morally wrong. But Hebrews 13:4 as translated in the *Complete Jewish Bible* says, "Marriage is honorable in every respect; and, in particular, sex within marriage is pure." That means that whatever a couple mutually desires to do sexually and within the context of marriage is God-endorsed. So, send flirty messages to one another. Tell your spouse what you'd like to do later when you get home. Be graphic. Be explicitly erotic. Write a short novel detailing how you will captivate your spouse when you're back together in the same room.

Psychology researchers reinforced the benefit of sexting for couples in a committed relationship. They found that it improves their sexual satisfaction, but also their overall happiness in the relationship. The same doesn't hold true for single people, where sexting has the opposite effect on sexual satisfaction as well as happiness (Andersen 2019).

Physical Intimacy Uses Active Communication

A leadership coach friend of ours said that many leaders don't get the kind of performance they want from their employees because they haven't been clear about what good performance looks like. The same holds true with physical intimacy. No one can read minds, so don't expect them to.

> *No one can read minds, so don't expect them to.*

"I Could Never Ask My Husband to Do That!"

A female client of ours enjoyed sex in a very specific way to achieve an orgasm. But she didn't feel like it was "proper," so she wouldn't tell her husband about the kind of sex she wanted. "It's just too embarrassing," she told us, "And I don't want to make my husband feel uncomfortable."

She avoided "making her husband feel uncomfortable" while still getting her sexual needs met. She had affairs with six different men who gave her exactly what she wanted.

If you were her spouse, would you rather hear something potentially "kinky," or have her find a half-dozen other men to meet her need?

I think we can all agree that open, honest communication would have been the way to go.

Instead of guessing, assuming, or mindreading, do this:

1. Ask your spouse questions and ask for feedback.
   - "Does that feel good?"
   - "Do you like that?"
   - "How can I drive you wild?"
   - "What feels best?"
   - "Should I continue? Should I stop?"

2. Tell your spouse specifically what you enjoy.
   - "Touch me right there."
   - "Kiss me, please."
   - "Be a little more gentle."
   - "I love it when you use your mouth."

3. Listen for nonverbal feedback.
   - Moans
   - Deep breaths
   - Panting
   - A wince

THE FOUR INTIMACIES

4. Debrief later.
- "Did anything feel especially good?"
- "Did anything not work for you?"
- "Is there something else you'd like me to try?"
- "What felt best for you?"

Does this sound too formulaic, unnatural, or even unnecessary? Perhaps to some. But if your spouse made a dinner that tasted awful, would you want to have it again next week? Of course not. And your spouse wouldn't want to make it for you if they knew you didn't enjoy it. Don't expect your spouse to "just know" what you thought about the meal. Saying nothing won't get you the outcome you want, either. By developing verbal and emotional intimacy, you can navigate conversations, regardless of whether the topic is about food or sexual desires.

Physical Intimacy Is Mutually Pleasurable and Reciprocated

Whereas porn is for masturbation (self-pleasure), physical intimacy involves mutual pleasure, one that culminates in two people feeling loved and fulfilled. If only one person comes away a "winner," both spouses lose in the long run. When physical intimacy isn't consensual and doesn't include verbal and emotional intimacy, a spouse can feel that sexual contact is more akin to marital rape than making love.

Some people with certain medical conditions can't achieve an orgasm, but that doesn't mean they can't experience physical intimacy. You can have physical intimacy in other ways:

- Holding hands
- Playing footsie
- Kissing
- Hugging
- Stroking hair
- Massaging

- Foot rubs
- Tickling
- Putting your arm around them when they sleep
- Placing your head on their shoulders
- Gazing into their eyes
- Rubbing their arm, patting their back, or squeezing their buttocks or thigh

The couples best at physical intimacy don't limit their definition to sexual intercourse or orgasm. Instead, they focus on providing pleasure to their spouses in ways that are unique to them.

Before doing your homework, let's return to the ten-point rating scale. Now that you've read more about what physical intimacy looks like and what the best couples do differently, we will ask you to re-evaluate your previous answer. Use the same scale: one (1) represents that you and your spouse have no physical intimacy, and ten (10) represents that you have so much physical intimacy that you skipped this chapter, finding it unnecessary. Circle the number that accurately corresponds with your current emotional intimacy level with your spouse.

1	2	3	4	5	6	7	8	9	10

Now you're ready to apply some best practices in physical intimacy.

Physical Intimacy Homework

First, what's your number? That's right, we all have a number, even if we've never shared that number aloud. And we're not talking about your phone number. We're asking how often do you want to have sex each year, month, or week?

THE FOUR INTIMACIES

While discussing a number sounds formulaic or lacking in spontaneity, it's critical that you express your desire with your spouse. If one says five times per week, and the other is five times per month, you will need a ton of work to find that middle ground. But it can be done. Remember, desire is not the same expectation. Working through the first two intimacies will help you bridge the gap.

If you find that you and your spouse have a huge desire difference, your next step is to use your verbal intimacy to discuss how to create physically intimate moments to meet each other's needs. For example, you can ask your spouse questions like the following:

- "Is there anything that I can do to increase your desire to make love more often?"
- "Are there things that I'm doing or not doing that reduce your desire for sexual intimacy?"
- "Are there specific times of day that you're more likely to be open to sexual intimacy?"
- "Are there duties I could take off your plate that would give you more energy to invest in our sexual relationship?"

Second, learn how to kiss—and we mean *really kiss*: slow, steady, and sensual for more than twenty seconds. What is it like to kiss for a full minute? Go ahead and set your timer. See if you can kiss for three minutes! What did you like, what didn't work, and what do you want to do again?

Finally, choose an area of each other's body to explore, as if for the first time, while continuously asking, "How does that feel? Do you enjoy it like this?" Over the years, our bodies and mindsets change. That's the one of the beauties of physical intimacy: that we can always be exploring.

Deeper Practice

Finally, fulfill your spouse, and then stop without reaching your own climax at that time. Here's how to do it….

Take thirty minutes or longer to pleasure your spouse sexually—and take them to climax. BUT, in this practice, talk to your spouse, ask questions about what feels good, etc. Ask your spouse to guide your moves, touches, kisses. Once your spouse is done, take a break. Don't get that sexual intimacy reciprocated.

The exercise is about providing 100 percent satisfaction to your spouse, not waiting your turn. Later that day or the next day, your spouse will do the same exercise for you.

Key Takeaways

- Physical intimacy involves using our bodies to become one by providing security and pleasure to each other.
- Physical intimacy is built when we make ourselves vulnerable and exposed fully to our spouse, surrender our sexual cravings to that of our spouse, prioritize the sexual needs of our spouse above our own, and practice physical intimacy exclusively with our spouse.
- The goal of *emotional* intimacy is for two people to *feel* as one. Physical intimacy moves that *feeling* into *physical embodiment* by giving ourselves sexually to loving our spouse.
- Pornography, or the "other woman," is the biggest obstacle to physical intimacy. Other barriers include carrying false beliefs, struggling to talk about sex, differing sex drives, and using sex as a weapon.

THE FOUR INTIMACIES

- Physical intimacy isn't just about sexual intercourse or climax. It includes intimate touching that's done only with our spouse.
- Strong physical intimacy improves our mental and physical health as well as reduces the risk of a broken relationship.
- Extraordinary physical intimacy begins with verbal and emotional intimacy. Getting better at asking, telling, nonverbal feedback, and debriefing leads to improved gratification and satisfaction.

We surrender our illusion of control, judgement, and understanding to experience a humble enlightenment.

CHAPTER 6

Spiritual Intimacy

Have you ever wondered if there was more to your relationship with God than what you have been currently experiencing? Maybe you've heard a story of someone who was so passionate and emotional about their experience with God, and you sit back and wonder, *What the heck happened to them? How did they get that, or get there?* Or, *Why hasn't that happened to me?*

Spiritual intimacy is the most abstract of all the intimacies, and we want to acknowledge that at the onset. Please do not skip this chapter. Our hope with spiritual intimacy is that when you unlock the first three intimacies, you will have a new and deeper spiritual experience and connection with each other.

Verbal intimacy deals with the spoken word, emotional intimacy involves feelings, and physical intimacy centers around touch. But what about spiritual intimacy? Depending on your background, the word *spiritual* may connote a religious belief system, formal spiritual dogma, communing with spirits, or anything else that resides outside of the physical world.

Spiritual intimacy is the only intimacy in which a third person is involved. It is the only time a third person can actually strengthen the relationship. One of the many beauties of God is that He is *for* our intimate relationship. This is His goal. In the beginning He saw all that He made, His entire incredible creation, and noticed that man was alone. And what did he say? "Not good". And so… He did something about it. He created the first intimate relationship.

Words to Know: Spiritual Intimacy

Spiritual intimacy involves becoming one as you experience the exponential results of applying verbal, emotional, and physical intimacies. In this fourth intimacy, we experience a oneness spiritually as we communicate with each other and God, become vulnerable emotionally, and obey God relationally with our bodies. Couples experience spiritual intimacy when they: (1) apply the first three intimacies and (2) pursue God together.

> *We surrender our illusion of control, judgement, and understanding to experience a humble enlightenment.*

As we have said before, each intimacy unlocks the next. Therefore, to experience spiritual intimacy you must apply and unlock the first three intimacies. The beauty of this process is that when you apply verbal, emotional and physical intimacy to your spiritual pursuit, you will have an intimate life with both your lover and your God.

Spiritual intimacy requires that you have vulnerable conversations with each other about who God is and what His desire is for your life. Be courageous and without judgement. Remember our key sentence: we ask questions and listen with an intent to understand and a willingness to be influenced. Ask your spouse questions about their faith and then just listen. Try to understand why they believe

THE FOUR INTIMACIES

what they believe. Allow yourself to be influenced by their thoughts and experiences. Likewise, to experience spiritual intimacy means that you also have those conversations with God. He is not afraid of your questions, and we bet He knows the answers.

Spiritual intimacy requires that you share and allow your emotions to be expressed and experienced in your pursuit of God. The Bible is filled with emotions and emotional people. We even read that God Himself is filled with passion and love and even anger. How can we have a true spiritual experience if we do not choose to implement our emotions within spiritual intimacy? When we share our emotions with each other, we begin to see and experience how God loves us emotionally. When we share our true emotions with God, we strengthen our relationship with Him as well.

How does physical intimacy strengthen our spiritual journey and experience? Have you ever had an orgasm and thought it was almost an out-of-body experience? Physical intimacy strengthens our spiritual journey when we realize that our bodies and the pleasure they experience are from God. He created us with these pleasures and senses in mind. The orgasm was His idea. We didn't invent it. What an amazing God to give us that. Can't you just hear Him saying, "Oh, they are going to love me for that one!"

As you pursue spiritual intimacy, we also encourage you to remember three primary characteristics of God: *1. God is bigger than us. 2. God is good and loving. 3. God is mysterious.*

First, regardless of your specific denomination, faith, or spiritual practice, understand that God is bigger than either you or your spouse. If God isn't bigger than you, then you imply that you are God. How can you be equals if you are your spouse's God or if your spouse tries to be your God? Likewise, if your God is smaller than you, then you will need to take on the weight of the world and try to solve all the problems on your own. This doesn't work well in an intimate relationship. Nobody can be truly intimate with someone who has a God complex.

Second, believing that God is good, and that He created you in His image, implies that you and your lover are good as well. Pursuing a God who is love and loving will set your mind with the right intention and belief about who you and your spouse truly are. You will then seek the positive in each other.

Third, believe that God is mysterious. When you do so, you will realize that you'll never have this spiritual stuff all figured out, just like you'll never have each other figured out. You're on a mysterious journey. Seeking and experiencing the mystery of God allows you to be non-judgmental and less dogmatic. When you treat your relationship like a mystery, you'll gain patience and understanding, since it takes a lifetime to unravel the depth and wonder of something so powerful.

Couples who achieve spiritual intimacy in this way can:

- Forgive one another
- Grow together
- Discuss deep and spiritual matters
- Put the other spouse first
- Build a shared purpose and goals
- Practice mutual encouragement and support
- Serve one another as well as others
- Bring out the best in one another
- Have a positive belief about each other
- Value the uniqueness of their spouse
- Contribute to a shared legacy
- Experience something bigger than themselves

Many world religions teach that "God is love." Spiritual intimacy mirrors that same love to our spouses—in all ways.

THE FOUR INTIMACIES

However, there's one caveat. Spiritual intimacy doesn't involve asking your spouse to save you, die for your sins, rise from the dead for you, or carry you. That's too much.

Based on our definition, how would you rate your level of spiritual intimacy with your spouse? Following is a ten-point rating scale. One (1) represents that you and your spouse have no spiritual intimacy, and ten (10) represents that you have so much spiritual intimacy that you live in continual communion with one another and God who draws you together. Circle the number that accurately corresponds with your current spiritual intimacy level with your spouse.

1	2	3	4	5	6	7	8	9	10

Just like with the other three intimacies, if you scored your current level at a lower number, don't be discouraged. Besides, this is the hardest intimacy to master. Read on, and we'll show you how.

Earlier in this book, we explained that the four intimacies must come in a specific order. Skip one, and the other types of intimacy may never develop fully. Many couples skip directly to physical intimacy to ensure they are "sexually compatible." When a female mastiff is in heat, even a male yorkie can resolve the mystery about sexual compatibility. Where there's a will—and maybe a step ladder—there's a way.

Views of Spirituality and Intimacy

On November 8, 1952, C.S. Lewis wrote: "It is Christ Himself, and not the Bible, who is the true word of God. The Bible, read in the right spirit and with the guidance of good teachers, will bring us to Him."

Martin Buber, a Jewish philosopher, wrote, "When two people relate to each other authentically and humanly, God is the electricity that surges between them" (Amodeo 2017).

In his book *Dancing with Fire: A Mindful Way to Loving Relationships,* John Amodeo writes, "Our spiritual quest receives its grounding through intimate connections, and at the same time, the fertile stream of spiritual practice nourishes our relationships."

Nearly all spiritual traditions and beliefs acknowledge that the height of connection comes from something beyond ourselves.

Do couples ever try to skip directly to spiritual intimacy, bypassing the other intimacies? In short, yes. People from various faiths often date and marry based on strong spiritual intimacy and compatibility. Devout believers from various faiths believe that following an identical spiritual dogma is the most critical element to a successful relationship. They would never consider entering a relationship with someone from a different faith or belief system, or even another denomination or specific congregation. An extreme example is the Shaker faith, a group that remained nearly completely celibate, even in marriage. They believed that any relationship without 100 percent focus on God was corrupt and inappropriate. Not surprisingly, the number of Shakers in the world has shrunk to two survivors (Blakemore 2017).

While we've never had a Shaker client, we've had several couples in therapy who tell us stories like this: "We love each other, and we love God. That's what brought us together and what keeps us together. We don't need frivolous conversations, airing our emotions, or any physical hanky-panky to be happy in our marriage."

However, when we separate the couple for individual counseling, we hear a different story: "I feel like I'm married to a nun, and not one of the wild ones like you see dressed up for Halloween. All she does is pray and read the Bible. I don't remember the last time we left the house together for anything besides church!"

To keep men from getting smug, we've also heard the same complaint from women who compare their husbands to priests or eunuchs: "I love that he prays so often, but I wish he'd talk to me, too. I need him to be my spouse, not act as my high priest. I like talking about heavenly things, but we also need to focus on the two of us. And I wouldn't mind something taking place beneath the sheets, either!"

We share stories about the "nun" and "priest" spouses for one reason: holy names and holy beliefs don't equate to spiritual intimacy. God didn't design couples to live like that. When one or both parties aspire to have a relationship built on "God only," both parties suffer from a lack of intimacy across the board.

Think about the last time you spent any amount of time with your extended family. As you sat down to eat, what conversation topic was likely to serve as an appetite suppressant and trigger for heated emotions? If you're like most families, the three topics you try to step around as if they were landmines are these:

- Politics
- Money
- Religion

And with good reason. Take politics. In America, there's about a 50 percent chance that the person sitting next to you stands in adamant opposition to your political beliefs. Politics isn't a safe topic in most settings.

Neither is talking about money. Who feels comfortable fielding questions like, "About how much do you make a year?" or hearing someone brag, "I remember when I was only making low six-figures, and I thought that was a lot of money back then…".

It's similar with religion. Less than 50 percent of the American population call themselves religious or are part of a congregation (Neuman 2021). Additionally, those who do practice religion have more than 4,000 faiths to choose from (National Day Calendar 2022).

If you don't feel comfortable discussing those topics at a family or work gathering, we don't blame you. And that isn't what we're suggesting. We aren't trying to help you build intimacy with your Uncle Wes who you see annually at Thanksgiving. We want you to live in full intimacy with your spouse.

Intimacy requires vulnerability, which calls for high-stakes, high-risk conversations where you expose a part of your soul that you don't share with anyone outside of your innermost circle. Intimacy means being open with your significant other. And spiritual intimacy requires openness about spiritual matters.

Building Spiritual Intimacy

Let's revisit Andrew and Beth, the couple living across the hall from Marty and Rachel. Unlike Marty and Rachel, who have gone their separate ways, Andrew and Beth continue to grow together. They have a stellar relationship.

Even though they have fantastic verbal, emotional, and physical intimacy, Andrew and Beth want more. They decide it's time to take the next step to make spiritual intimacy a regular part of their relationship.

To do so, Andrew and Beth have established Wednesday night as their time to talk. But they don't discuss chores, bills, or where to eat. Instead, this is a time they've set aside to probe each other on deeper issues that fall on the spiritual plane. Following is a list of questions that Andrew and Beth came up with together. Each Wednesday, they pick a topic and talk about it until they've explored one another's beliefs, values, and thoughts on the subject. Here's a look at their list:

What I Want to Know Is...?

- If you didn't have to work, what charity or cause would you invest your time in? Why?
- What is the number one way you show love *to* someone you care about?
- What is the number one way you wish to receive love *from* someone you care about?
- What do you consider your life's purpose?
- What situation in your life has led to your greatest growth?
- What was your experience with religion as a child and young adult?
- Do you think there's a God? Why or why not?
- What do you know about God?
- Do you think we get punished for doing wrong and rewarded for doing right?
- What do you think happens to us when we die?
- Are you afraid to die?
- Do you believe in ghosts? Do you believe that alien life exists?
- If you knew for certain that God was real, would you live your life any differently than you do now?
- If you could ask God any question, what would you want to know?
- What is the hardest thing you've had to forgive another person for? How did you do it?
- At the end of your life, what do you want people to say about you as they celebrate your life? What do you want them not to say?
- What do you want to leave behind as your greatest contribution for having been here on Earth?
- What does it mean to give your life to God or Jesus?
- What does it mean to be "Born Again"?

Does that sound like a long list? Perhaps, but these questions just scratch the surface of developing spiritual intimacy. In most relationships, discussions like this can lead to two or three additional questions.

Have you had conversations like this with your spouse? If yes, good for you for initiating deeper, more intimate conversations with your spouse. If not, that's okay. You'll see them again later in this chapter.

How Do We Get Spiritual Intimacy Wrong?

Second Corinthians 6:14 in the *Amplified Bible* says, "Do not be unequally bound together with unbelievers [do not make mismatched alliances with them, inconsistent with your faith]." While this quote comes from the *New Testament* of the *Christian Bible*, the truth applies universally to couples in a relationship when one or both parties have a strong religious faith. If one spouse practices a belief system when the other does not, or if the spouses have different views on faith, couples can find themselves in conflict. Many times, conflict first appears when the couple is expecting their first child and discussing which faith the child should be raised in.

Couples can run into other problems when it comes to exploring and living their faiths in a relationship. Following are the ones we hear most commonly in therapy.

My Spiritual Practices Are Stronger Than Yours

We've never had a couple come to us with this problem: "My wife says she likes pizza. But I don't see evidence of that. I LOVE pizza. I eat it all the time. I feel like she's not into pizza as much as I am, and it's causing a huge rift in our relationship." Yet we know of multiple relationships wherein a spouse will substitute the words *spiritual practices* for *pizza*. We could write a book on that one topic alone.

THE FOUR INTIMACIES

In most relationships, it's usual that one spouse will possess a greater need to discuss and share parts of their spiritual journey than the other. The problem comes when one spouse believes their faith is stronger or better than that of their spouse. This can lead to judging or comparing the relative strengths of their faiths, instead of inspiring curiosity about the elements they have in common.

Early in his marriage, Jim started dreading Saturday nights with his wife, Linda. After they finished watching *Saturday Night Live*, Linda would invariably ask, "So, are you coming to church with me tomorrow?"

Sigh, Jim groaned to himself. *Here we go again.*

"It's been a really long week," he'd usually say, "and I have things around the house I need to catch up on."

"You say that every week," Linda reprimanded him. "Are you ever going to go to church again?"

When they first got married, they attended a church at their local parish where they would sing, listen to the priest talk, and take part in the Eucharist. But a year later, Jim started to question his faith. After suffering an emotional setback in his life due to the death of a close friend, the priest shared a cliché with him about sorrow and suffering. That turned Jim off completely. The priest's lack of empathy made Jim question his Catholic upbringing. *If the priest represents God on Earth, does that mean God doesn't care, either?* he wondered. After that, Jim started dodging mass.

Linda viewed her spiritual practices as stronger than that of her church-avoiding husband. Jim, on the other hand, would love to talk with Linda about his crisis of faith, but when he had shared some of his internal conflict in the past, he felt judged by his wife.

At an impasse, Linda continued going to church, and Jim continued staying home. Eventually, Linda gave Jim the silent treatment for the remainder of each Sunday after she came home.

To no one's surprise, their marriage didn't last.

My Spiritual Practices Are Superior to Yours

We don't know of any religions that elevate pride and arrogance as a sign of devotion. Yet some couples argue that the depth of their faith, the level of participation or the understand of their beliefs are superior. Nothing sours intimacy like placing yourself above your spouse.

Viewed from a higher level, can you think of a spiritual faith that doesn't promote forgiveness, growth, continuous learning, worship, selflessness, purpose, encouragement, service, and contribution?

My Spiritual Beliefs Are Private

Some adhere to the previously shared belief that religious or spiritual topics shouldn't be discussed, even with their spouses. In most cases, this comes from a bad experience of sharing their beliefs in the past, and they don't want to risk an argument, disagreement, or ridicule. The topic becomes taboo.

Imagine sitting in a class, listening to a professor's lecture. She says something provocative that you've never thought of before, so you shoot up your hand to ask a follow up question.

"Sorry, no questions," she replies with a wave of her hand.

Without asking questions, how can you learn more? Without a discussion, how can you test your ideas and gain greater insight?

If a professor treated you like this, in the short term, you'd stop asking questions. Over time, even though her lectures interested you, you'd realize that the professor wasn't invested in going deeper or expanding your knowledge, since discussion is off limits. Eventually, you might stop listening or drop the class.

Similarly, when couples don't discuss spiritual matters with one another, their ability to grow spiritually towards one another is hampered. Think of spiritual intimacy as a process, not a destination. Its ongoing nature means that couples developing spiritual intimacy perpetually learn more about one another, find paths that they can walk together, and establish goals that they can share.

> *Think of spiritual intimacy as a process, not a destination.*

Benefits of Spiritual Intimacy

Couples with spiritual intimacy report greater individual well-being, life satisfaction, and perceived psychological and physical health (Holland et al. 2016, 218–27). Research from Bowling Green State University found that spiritual intimacy in a marriage offers some additional benefits over couples lacking spiritual intimacy (BGSU 2022). Couples with a high level of spiritual intimacy experience:

- Greater warmth, humor, and love for one another
- Less negativity and hostility toward one another
- Greater marital satisfaction

In their book *Becoming Soul Mates,* authors and spouses Les and Leslie Parrott put it this way: "Developing our spiritual intimacy is the foundation for a lasting marriage...It's the feeling of freedom that you can connect at any time and in any way about spiritual matters or issues. There is no walking on eggshells about sharing or raising a question. You live your lives in the confidence that you are connected spiritually" (Parrott and Parrott 1995, 164).

One word that comes up wherever intimacy is discussed is *connection*. So far, we've written about building a verbal, emotional, and physical connection with your spouse. If you've ever seen a stone archway and marveled at how it stays secure, the answer is the wedge-shaped stone at the top called a keystone. That keystone places equal pressure on both sides of the archway walls, locking the structure in place. In the same way, the spiritual connection you have with your spouse is a keystone that strengthens all other intimacies.

Best Practices in Spiritual Intimacy

High school debate team members and lawyers want to be right. That's their objective. They view the person on the other side of the table as an opponent to be dispatched with logic, facts, and hard evidence.

Obviously, that's not how couples build spiritual intimacy. When a discussion turns into a debate or an argument, both parties lose, and intimacy is weakened instead of strengthened. Spiritual intimacy is the process of sharing and listening to spiritual disclosure within a safe, judgment-free relationship.

From research and our experiences counseling couples, following are the practices that the best couples do differently than the rest.

Normalizing and Prioritizing Spiritual Discussions

In the article "9 Conversations Every Couple Needs to Have," author Ruth Soukup writes about topics like money, pet peeves, life goals, and end-of-life-care. And faith. Soukup says this: "[B]y allowing our faith to shape and strengthen our marriage, by praying together, attending services, or discussing our beliefs, we keep our marriage a spiritual journey and connection, beyond just the physical and emotional" (Soukup 2020).

The best couples openly discuss where they are on their own spiritual journeys. They ask one another questions and even share their doubts with each other.

If a couple has never had a frank conversation about what they like or dislike in their physical intimacy, it's awkward at first. And if you've never had a deep, spiritual conversation about your beliefs and faith, expect it to feel just as clumsy. But it's worth the effort.

Worshipping Together

When you think of worship, you probably picture a church, synagogue, temple, mosque, or some other structure that houses people for the purpose of growing their collective faiths. Beyond the overt spiritual benefits of worshiping together, attending services with your spouse also provides socialization with others who are interested in growing. Many find attending formal worship heightens their gratitude, instills their hearts with reverence, gives back to others, promotes forgiveness, and connects them to deeper meaning.

If you don't like the idea of taking part in formal worship, consider spending time Sunday morning walking on the beach or in the woods with your spouse. You can achieve some of the same benefits of worship if you share with your spouse the things you're grateful for. You can sing together, talk about the best parts of your relationship, or have a deeper discussion about the meaning of life.

Worship simply involves diverting your eyes from yourselves and putting them on something bigger than you. Whether worshiping God in church or lifting your eyes up to the majesty of nature around you, couples who spend time looking for meaning together often find it.

French writer Antoine de Saint-Exupéry said, "Love does not consist in gazing at each other, but in looking outward together in the same direction."

We cannot think of a better description of worship in spiritual intimacy.

Pray Together

Here's what research on prayer says:

- When you pray for your spouse, even when you feel tension in your marriage, both spouses report greater relationship satisfaction.
- People who see God as a spouse in life experience better mental and physical health.
- Prayer makes people feel emotionally supported.
- Prayer as a form of spiritual meditation calms the central nervous system at a greater level than secular meditation (APS 2020).

The most well-known Christian prayer, "The Lord's Prayer," is recited by people of all faiths, and it's a standard feature at most twelve-step recovery meetings. It says,

> Our Father, in heaven, hallowed be Your name; Your kingdom come; Your will be done on earth as it is in heaven. Give us this day our daily bread; and forgive us our debts as we forgive our debtors; and lead us not into temptation, but deliver us from evil. For Yours is the kingdom and the power and glory forever. Amen.

Did you notice the first word? *Our.* In those sixty-two words, the words *our*, *us*, and *we* appear nine times. This prayer demonstrates unity and alignment of purpose and intentions.

Regardless of the prayer used, prayer unifies couples. As the saying goes, "A couple that prays together stays together." Prayer allows couples to share in a spiritual story and journey.

Leaning into One Another and onto Something Beyond Yourselves

The real test of a relationship's strength comes in times of crisis and heartbreak. Kenneth Pargament, professor emeritus in the psychology department at Bowling Green State University, said it this way: "There may still be some atheists in foxholes. But the general trend is for the religious impulse to quicken in a time of crisis" (Sax et al. 2020).

We can think of no sadder scenario than a couple losing a child. Unfortunately, losses such as this are just as likely to pull couples apart as bring them closer together. This makes sense. Two broken, grieving parents can lean on one another, but the weight of grief is often more than they can bear. That's when turning to God offers comfort and strength, especially when a couple does so together.

Leaning on God

When his eighteen-year-old daughter, Alana, from a previous marriage died from a drug overdose, Scott broke into pieces. As a recovering alcoholic, Scott wanted to return to alcohol to numb his pain. Within an hour, he entered a bar and ordered a drink, while his wife and Alana's stepmother, Jocelyn, reeling from her own grief, stood behind him silently praying. Scott left the bar without touching his drink.

On the flight back home, Scott raged about his daughter's death, threatening revenge on every person who had played a hand in her death. Jocelyn wept and continued to pray silently.

When Scott woke up screaming in anguish, Jocelyn hugged him, wept alongside him, and prayed for him.

At their daughter's funeral, Jocelyn prayed for Scott's strength and willingness to let God speak through him.

As Scott stood behind the podium to address the audience that included hundreds of his daughter's friends, many of them struggling with their own addictions, he shared a message that pointed everyone to something bigger than the death of his own precious daughter.

> If you were one of Alana's friends, you are welcome here. If you partied with Alana and enjoyed her as "the life of the party," you are welcome here. If you introduced Alana to heroin, or if you drove her to buy heroin, or you used heroin with Alana, you most certainly are welcome here. And I'd like to talk with you. And I'd like you to know that I love you. And I'd like you to know that Alana loved you. And if you knew Alana at all, you knew that she would have laid down her life for you.
>
> Don't listen to the sweet lies of addiction that tell you that it's too late for you turn back. It isn't. As long as there is life, there is hope. Tonight you can find a loving community of support to help you on your way to recovery and to life, the life that you know you can live, the life Alana would want you to live.
>
> You don't have to live like Alana—terrified, defeated, and alone. And you don't have to die like Alana, either. Please make Alana's death mean something. She would have given everything to be part of your recovery and healing.

Leaning on his relationship with God and the support of his wife, Scott moved hundreds of the mourners to tears by pointing them to something bigger: hope, forgiveness, recovery, and healing. Within two weeks of Alana's funeral, six of her friends entered recovery. Had Scott not leaned on something bigger than himself, his grief and brokenness may have led him to deliver a very different message that night. After this tragic event, Scott and Jocelyn began working to help others into recovery as part of their shared spiritual practice.

Spiritual Intimacy Homework

Author Brian Tracy said, "The hardest part of any important task is getting started on it in the first place. Once you actually begin work on a valuable task, you seem to be naturally motivated to continue."

Building spiritual intimacy is important to the health and depth of a relationship. It's worth the effort. The hardest part, of course, is getting started, especially if this hasn't been part of your practice as a couple.

To help you get started, take a minute to answer the following questions developed by Bowling Green State University for measuring spiritual intimacy for psychological research. Section 1 is for you to complete about your own spiritual feelings. Section 2 is based on your feelings about your spouse's spiritual feelings.

Talk with your spouse before taking the survey, and agree to a set amount of time to discuss the answers. When you're ready, take a couple of minutes to complete Section 1 (about yourself). Write yes, no, or sometimes next to each question. There are no right or wrong answers, nor is there a rating scale.

Section 1: My Personal Feelings on Spiritual Intimacy

_____ I feel safe being completely open and honest with my spouse about my faith.

_____ I tend to keep my spiritual side private and separate from my marriage.

_____ I try not to be judgmental or critical when my spouse shares his/her ideas about spirituality.

_____ I try to be supportive when my spouse discloses spiritual questions or struggles.

Once you've completed Section 1, follow the same process in Section 2 (what you feel about your spouse).

Section 2: My Feelings about My Spouse Regarding Spiritual Intimacy

_____ My spouse shares his/her spiritual questions or struggles with me.

_____ My spouse doesn't disclose his/her thoughts or feelings about spirituality with me.

_____ My spouse really knows how to listen when I talk about my spiritual needs, thoughts, and feelings.

_____ My spouse is supportive when I reveal my spiritual questions or struggles to them.

Once you've both completed Section 1 and 2, discuss your responses with your spouse, while practicing these safe behaviors:

1. **Don't judge.** The survey requires vulnerability. This discussion should not devolve into an argument or debate with your spouse. Commit to making this conversation a safe place.
2. **Don't take the results personally.** The survey is designed to capture a snapshot of your feelings at a specific moment in time. Answer the same questions next week, and the results may be different. Instead

of getting defensive with what your spouse shares with you, use what you hear to evaluate yourself for how you can provide greater spiritual intimacy moving forward.

Deeper Practice

Let's return to the list (below) of conversation-starting questions from Andrew and Beth. Before beginning, look at the ground rules listed beneath the "What I Want to Know Is...?" list.

As you'll see from the list, the first questions require less vulnerability and have less spiritual content.

What I Want to Know Is...?

Warm-Up Questions

- If you didn't have to work, what charity or cause would you invest your time in? Why?
- What is the number one way you show love *to* someone you care about?
- What is the number one way you wish to receive love *from* someone you care about?
- What do you consider your life's purpose?
- What situation in your life has led to your greatest growth?
- Do you believe in ghosts? Do you believe that alien life exists?
- What was your experience with religion as a child and young adult?

Moderate Questions

- What is the hardest thing you've had to forgive another person for? How did you do it?
- What do you know about God?
- Do you think there's a God? Why or why not?
- Do you pray? If so, what do you pray about?

- Do you think we get punished for doing wrong and rewarded for doing right?
- Who is Jesus?

Deeper Questions

- What do you think happens to us when we die?
- Are you afraid to die?
- If you knew for certain that God was real, would you live your life any differently than you do now?
- If you could ask God any question, what would you want to know?
- Would you feel comfortable praying with me?
- At the end of your life, what do you want people to say about you as they celebrate your life? What do you want them not to say?
- What do you want to leave behind as your greatest contribution for having been here on Earth?

Ground rules for the deeper practice:

- Schedule a time to talk with your spouse about spiritual matters.
- Start with a predetermined time limit of twenty to thirty minutes.
- Read one question aloud.
- Take turns responding to the question, asking each other questions, and letting the conversation take its own course.
- Remain judgment-free about anything your spouse shares.
- Ask clarifying or follow-up questions to provoke more information from your spouse.
- When you're done, thank your spouse for making spiritual intimacy a priority.
- Spend some time in physical intimacy as outlined in the previous chapter.

Remember that this conversation has nothing to do with being right, making a case for your beliefs, or getting your spouse to take your side. It's about sharing your spiritual thoughts, some of which you might not have discussed with another person. The objective is to connect on a higher plane, find commonality, and build on a similar spiritual foundation as your intimacy continues to grow.

Key Takeaways

- Spiritual intimacy is the culmination of experiencing the other three intimacies.
- Couples experiencing spiritual intimacy pursue a God who is bigger than themselves, good, and mysterious. As a result, they spend time in worship together.
- Couples acting in spiritual intimacy treat one another like one would imagine the kindest God would treat others, which includes forgiving one another.
- Spiritual intimacy isn't about "converting" anyone to a particular dogma, faith, or belief system. Instead, it's about growing together in purpose.
- Couples who achieve the highest level of spiritual intimacy worship and pray together as well as lean on each other and something bigger than themselves in difficult times. They also report higher marital satisfaction than those who don't practice spiritual intimacy.

Gratitude is the foundation for life.

Ch 7 Summary

CHAPTER 7

Keeping the Intimate Love Unlocked

Think of the four intimacies as a hierarchy.

We get to know people through verbal conversation. Most relationships start with a simple conversation that includes questions like:

- "What's your name?"
- "Where are you from?"
- "Where do you work?"
- "Do you want to grab a cup of coffee?"

(Pyramid diagram, top to bottom: Spiritual Intimacy / Physical Intimacy / Emotional Intimacy / Verbal Intimacy)

As a relationship grows, the depth of conversation grows, too.

Verbal intimacy leads to emotional intimacy, where two people become increasingly vulnerable with one another, sharing parts of their lives that transcend casual conversations. Instead of exchanging words, couples feel safe in expressing their innermost feelings.

When a couple feels safe exchanging words and emotions, their relationship can be unlocked to experience physical intimacy. Their vulnerability moves into a physical manifestation of trust.

With verbal intimacy, you share thoughts; with emotional intimacy, you share feelings; and with physical intimacy, you share security and pleasure. But with spiritual intimacy, you share deep, abstract thoughts about faith, purpose, and what lies beyond the physical world. Sharing spiritual intimacy takes you to the height of vulnerability and risk. It also requires the most faith and can be met with generations of authority, indifference, resistance, or even ridicule.

Each level of intimacy comes with its own challenges, as we've shared in this book. The strongest couples push past any discomfort, baggage from past relationships, or old habits, to develop intimacy with each other. The couples that accomplish this enjoy a level of marital satisfaction and closeness that others long for.

The Soulmate Myth

A 2011 study conducted by Marist found that 73 percent of Americans believe in the concept of a one-and-only soulmate, the idea that each of us has a perfect spouse out there in the world (Polanchek and Shaw 2019). As enticing as this belief is, it defies logic. With a population of 7.75 billion people spanning the globe, the idea of finding your one-and-only soulmate is romantic but not realistic.

The tallest building in the world today is the Burj Khalifa in Dubai. The mixed-use building has the capacity to hold ten thousand people. If you lived there, what are the chances that you would meet everyone in the building? If you can't know everyone in just that one building, what are the odds that you can find your one in 7,750,000,000 somewhere on the globe?

Another pitfall of the one-and-only soulmate idea, also known as a destiny belief, is the assumption that once you meet that special someone, your relationship will be perfect (Brooks 2022). Anyone in a relationship knows this to be false. Relationships take work, and developing intimacy requires even more effort.

Despite the challenges, developing intimacy is worth the investment. We change and grow throughout our lifetimes. Our thoughts, feelings, and sexual impulses don't remain constant. Nor should our spiritual lives remain fixed. Sharing our spiritual beliefs, questions, and doubts with our spouse allows us to explore the greatest mysteries of life.

Why Does Intimacy Require Perpetual Effort?

If I asked you to drive from Florida to Maine without stopping for gas, you'd think I was a lunatic. However, we meet with couples all the time who want an extraordinary intimate relationship but never want to stop and "fuel up." Or they try practicing the four intimacies but wonder why it wears off. If you want to make progress, fueling up isn't a one-time event.

Intimacy is your relationship's fuel. When you plan to be with someone for a short time, like on a date, you don't need a deep reserve. Anyone can be on their best behavior for an hour-long dinner. But when you're planning to be with someone for a lifetime, you must keep your intimacy fueled. Otherwise, the relationship won't go the distance.

Humans are ever-changing. Let's say you married at age twenty. Are you the same person at thirty that you were at twenty? How about forty? Fifty? Of course not! Your wants and needs change. You may or may not have had kids. You've likely changed jobs at least a few times, and you may have moved to new homes or entirely new states or even countries as the years pass. You therefore don't want a spouse who continues to meet the needs you had at twenty, if those needs have changed. You want a spouse who understands how intimacy morphs, grows, and shifts throughout every stage of life. And that requires regular effort and investment.

A lasting relationship is a lifelong adventure, not a two-week vacation. When people take a vacation, they post the highlight reel on social media along with a caption like, "My honey and I got to swim with this dolphin!" That's a highlight, something you'll need when you get so frustrated with your spouse that you picture pushing them into a pool of sharks.

The deeper your intimacy is with your spouse, the more you'll appreciate your investment in your lifelong adventure. Intimacy tells you that a difference of opinion isn't terminal. Intimacy warms you even when your spouse hogs the blanket. Intimacy stays close to you when you have to be apart. It comforts you when you're down, and it laughs with you when your heart leaps for joy. It celebrates with you, cries with you, and looks to the future with you. Intimacy always seeks the best in you.

Say Yes to the Lifelong Adventure

The television show *Say Yes to the Dress* has aired since 2007. On the show, a New York-based bridal salon does whatever is in their power to create magic and perfection for brides-to-be. During nineteen seasons and more than three hundred episodes, viewers tune in to see a bride find the perfect dress for her wedding day.

In most cases, a wedding happens within one day. When the salon owners want a bride-to-be to say "yes" to a certain dress, it will only be worn for one part of that day. It won't be worn again unless it's sold or handed down to the next generation…one dress for one part of one day.

A wedding, in theory, is a one-time event. Yet a committed, intimate relationship is a lifetime. What fills in this gap between "one day" and "forever"?

"Happily ever after" has nothing to do with wedding invitations, guest lists, dresses, cakes, reception halls, photographers, bridal parties, first dances, walks down the aisle, chicken or fish, or ceremonies. Happily ever after requires that spouses make continuous investments in building, growing, nurturing, and holding sacred their intimacy.

Long after dresses, photos, and memories fade, spouses who invest in intimacy will see their relationship grow brighter.

Special Circumstances

While we've addressed many scenarios in this book, we realize there are more. This section will explore some additional special circumstances we hear about in our counseling sessions.

What if My Spouse Isn't Interested in Building the Four Intimacies?

When counseling clients, we frequently hear something like this: "I want to build intimacy with my spouse. But they aren't interested. They say that I need to fix myself if I want a stronger relationship, but they aren't interested in changing anything on their side. What do I do?"

Be honest with yourself: is this something that you could hear your spouse saying as you read this book? Something like, "Go ahead. But I'm not going to be involved"? If you answered yes, we're deeply sorry for you and your relationship. As we shared in the first chapter, relationships are built on the three legs of *time*, *trust*, and *communication*. The seat that connects those legs into something useful and strong is *reciprocity*. When a spouse says, "Go ahead and do it alone," that removes the seat. Without reciprocity, a relationship takes on the dynamic of master and servant, which conjures up many different images—none of them loving.

An unwilling spouse doesn't create a recipe for a happy, healthy, intimate relationship. But there are some things you can do.

Work on Yourself. Having evaluated your satisfaction level on the verbal, emotional, physical, and spiritual intimacy with your spouse, you've heightened your awareness about your feelings. You know what's working and what's not.

Now focus on only *your* actions that contributed to any dissatisfaction with your spouse for each of the four intimacies. In the areas where you have low satisfaction, ask yourself these two questions, and write down your thoughts as they come to you:

1. *In what way do my own behaviors contribute to these scores?*

2. *What am I currently doing on my side of the relationship to improve the level of satisfaction for both of us?*

If you find that you have unresolved bitterness, resentment, and hostility towards your spouse that keeps you from building intimacy together, start there. Admit it to yourself and your spouse. Seek forgiveness from your spouse. Determine a plan of action to fill the gaps that you helped to create. Tell your spouse the ways you intend to make changes to improve the relationship. Ask your spouse what more you can do to demonstrate your desire to foster intimacy.

THE FOUR INTIMACIES

Lead with Questions. If you're already doing everything to grow your relationship and build intimacy with your spouse, don't nag or whine. If your spouse doesn't want to put forth the effort to grow your relationship and intimacy, asking questions of your spouse is a more effective way to learn things that perhaps you can't see on your own.

Tell your spouse that you'd like to talk. Schedule a time.

Throughout this book, we've suggested that you schedule times to build intimacy. This is another one of those times. Scheduling a time to talk makes it clear that what you wish to discuss can't be ripped through during a commercial break.

Then come prepared with specific questions like these:

- "Are you satisfied with our relationship?"
- "Are there things that you wish worked better between us?"
- "What do you want out of our relationship?"
- "How do you see us moving forward through the years?"
- "What does your ideal relationship include? What doesn't it include?"
- "What can I do to make it better? What are you willing to do to make it better?"

Asking these questions and listening without judgment does a couple of things.

First, it shows your spouse that the relationship is important to you. Couples rarely schedule time for anything unless it's important. If you wished to take a vacation with your spouse, you'd make time to discuss possible destinations, dates, and activities to explore. The outcome of a conversation on your relationship vision has greater significance for your relationship's long-term health than if you visit the beaches of Florida or mountains of Colorado.

Second, this gives your spouse a chance to share their feelings. You might think you know how your spouse feels, but asking and listening to their answers removes the possibility for projecting your own feelings onto your spouse or having to play the role of a mind reader. Asking and listening shows respect, and it is the opposite of telling and accusing them of not being invested in your relationship.

Finally, asking questions and listening with the intent to understand and a willingness to be influenced, gives you an idea about your next move. Maybe your spouse is willing to work on your relationship to build intimacy, and this conversation surfaced some obstacles that must first be overcome. Or it might verify something for you: it's possible that *you're both good people but in the wrong relationship.*

Know Your Limit. Once you've done your own work and talked with your spouse about their vision for your relationship, the next decision is up to you. Your decision comes down to two bipolar choices: continue to invest, or move on.

We know that evaluating these two extreme positions requires substantial time and emotional energy. You must process, decide, and act upon the outcome. The decision gets even more complicated if you have young children, insufficient finances, or other special circumstances to factor in.

If you've reached the point in your relationship where you're considering leaving, you likely already realize that staying is the easiest course of action. Staying is known. You already know how to live in an unfulfilling relationship.

The fear comes from our thoughts like: *What happens if I leave? What happens if this relationship is as good as it gets for me? What happens if I leave and die alone? What if he/she does great in their next relationship? Then were the problems all mine?*

Counselor and authors Dr. Henry Cloud and Dr. John Townsend say it this way: "We change our behavior when the pain of staying the same becomes greater than the pain of changing."

Ending a relationship, whether breaking up or getting a divorce, is painful for many reasons. That's why we don't skip immediately to ending a relationship as the answer, except when the relationship includes abuse. Every relationship and spouse in every relationship is different. When we counsel individuals, we know their history and their relationship. Even with all of the information in front of us, we don't lightly recommend terminating a relationship. That's something only the client can conclude.

But if you as a reader are considering ending a relationship with your spouse, answer these questions of yourself:

If I stay in my current relationship:

1. *Can I see myself living like this for the rest of my life?*
2. *What is the best I can expect and hope for?*
3. *Will I become bitter and resentful when I don't receive reciprocated love and intimacy?*
4. *Will I be more likely to seek intimacy with someone who isn't my spouse?*
5. (If you have children) *How will this impact and shape the lives of my children?*

Efforts and Expectations

If you want a dynamic, growing, intimate relationship, ask yourself: *do my efforts match my expectations?* Don't expect to get what you don't give.

In our one-on-one counseling sessions with clients, we frequently ask dissatisfied spouses if their efforts match their expectations. It's easy to have huge expectations for "happily ever after" and living in the fairytale relationship. But it's sometimes apparent that the spouse with the highest expectations puts in a lower level of effort to make that dream a reality.

> *Don't expect to get what you don't give.*

If you're not satisfied with your current level of intimacy with your spouse, ask yourself: *Am I investing enough to get the return I want?* Work to become the person you want to be with.

If your efforts do match your expectations and you're still dissatisfied, it might be time to ask your spouse, "Can you share with me the ways you're investing into our relationship?"

There may be efforts that have been overlooked or misunderstood. Understanding your Love Language here will help.

I'm Not in a Relationship; How Can I Use What I've Read to Find a Great One?

Dating can be intimidating. It requires that you "put yourself out there" to a stranger to see if there's any possible connection. In addition to dressing for the date and checking yourself in the mirror countless times, you put on the best version of yourself. This probably includes a polished persona that appears calm, funny, agreeable, and likeable. And you might be all of those things! But just like a profile picture on social media, this is the *best* version of you, not the just-rolled-out-of-bed version.

If you want to find a spouse who grows to enjoy and love you, don't show up with a watered-down or compromised version of yourself on the inside. Don't lower your standards. Don't settle. Your authentic self is the only one that will receive and experience the love they long for.

Raise Your Standards

We love this quote by Mandy Hale, the bestselling author of *The Single Woman*: "Once you raise your standards, only the boys will disappear. The men will step up to meet them."

THE FOUR INTIMACIES

Create the list of character traits that are non-negotiable for your next relationship. If you don't see them demonstrated while you're dating, don't expect them to appear once you get married. Know your deal-breakers.

Also know your must-haves, which are different for everyone. These represent your standards. When you date someone, evaluate them against your list.

Use the following as a guide to help you start developing your own list.

Must-Haves	Deal-Breakers
Kindness	Anger issues/abuse
Vulnerability	Dishonesty
Respect, instills value	Infidelity
Affection	Emotional distance
Strong work ethic	Addiction
Confidence	Arrogance
God-seeking	Self-centered

Remember as you pursue a new relationship that the four intimacies are meant to follow a specific order for good reason: they build upon one another. Bypassing verbal or emotional intimacy to jump into physical intimacy might mean your relationship never develops the requisite intimacies. Once you establish verbal and emotional intimacy, physical intimacy develops as a natural outcome. Skipping to spiritual intimacy based on your deeply shared faith might result in you becoming best friends without a physical spark.

Finally, if you start a relationship that doesn't work out, don't blame yourself. Many clients, especially women, tend to assume responsibility to "fix" things in a relationship by giving up their identity. *If I just let go of this one part of myself or lower my standards to accept their deal-breaker, I can make the relationship work*, they reason. That's a recipe for lifelong discontent. Instead, be willing to say to yourself: *great person, wrong relationship*.

How to Deepen Your Intimacy Now

If you and your spouse both desire to deepen your intimacy, complete the exercises in this book. Some can be done together, and others are to be worked alone. Once you've compared notes, you're ready for the work that will continue as long as your relationship continues. In this section, we'll leave you with some final strategies to reinforce the four intimacies you've learned about.

Create Your Relationship Vision

Your *relationship vision* is your desired aspirational identity for yourselves as a couple.

Let's break down each component of a relationship vision.

First, a relationship vision is something both spouses want. Growing intimacy in a relationship is too critical to leave to chance or to say, "Let's just see what happens." It starts with a strong desire for personal, relational, and spiritual growth. This desire is mutually shared, without one spouse carrying both parties.

Second, a relationship vision is aspirational. It's what you wish to achieve and accomplish in your relationship, not what you currently have achieved. It's what you're working towards. Remember the old saying about valuing progress, not perfection? View your intimacy as an ongoing work in progress.

Third, a relationship vision is like having your own brand. When people say Nike or Chanel or Hermes, they have an idea what that brand is all about—all kinds of components, one brand. Even though there are two of you, think of how to become one brand. What do you stand for? What do you like to do? When people say, "Have you met Kim and Peter? They are so…(fill in the blank)," what do you want them to say? Decide who you want to be together, and give it to the world.

We shared earlier in the book that building intimacy in a relationship doesn't involve losing your own identity. However, it does require that you create an identity as a couple that is distinct from your identity as an individual.

As a couple, answer the following questions to develop your unique relationship vision:

1. *What defines our relationship? What are the main characteristics that we're known for as a couple?*
2. *How do we wish others to describe our relationship? What do we want them to say and feel after spending time with us?*
3. *What "relationship brand" do we want to create?*
4. *How do we want to grow together?*

Review and update your relationship vision regularly. Evaluate how well you're doing on living your relationship vision. Ask yourself if any obstacles exist in your relationship that must be removed to realize your vision.

Live in Gratitude

Gratitude is the foundation for life. There are two states of being in regards to gratitude: you are either cultivating gratitude, or allowing criticism to take root. This is especially true in our intimate relationships. When we stop looking for positive qualities and expressing gratitude towards our spouse, criticism springs up like a weed to take its place.

Your spouse can be an endless catalyst for your gratitude. You can show it through statements like:

- "Thank you for sharing your thoughts with me—sometimes random ones, other times profound ones."
- "I love when you share your emotions with me, opening up about both the successes you're experiencing as well as the trials."
- "You know me fully and love me anyway."
- "You put a smile on my face and a spring in my step."
- "You make me feel safe being myself."
- "The way you love me helps me love myself"
- "You know how to turn me on, I'm crazy about you."
- Your more beautiful today than the day I met you."
- "Thank you for dreaming with me and believing we can do anything."
- "You give me reason to believe in something that is bigger, good, and mysterious."
- "You are my unique love and an extension of the best parts of me."
- "I love us and who we are."
- "I love the way you love me."

Unlocking Love Every Day

Change can happen overnight or it can take a while. Our hope is that as you read this book you will slowly share and apply all that you have read. Please be patient with yourself and especially with others.

Remember how clueless we thought Marty was? Think again...

Rachel: "Marty? Is that really you? Wow, you look fantastic,"
Marty "Hey, Rachael, how've you been? What's it been, six months?"
Rachel: "Oh, Marty, I think it's been nine, maybe ten," .
Marty: "Sorry, I've been really busy."
Rachel: "Well, you look great, what have you been up to?"
Marty: "A lot," Marty sighs with a smile. "Yeah, after we split, I had to take

THE FOUR INTIMACIES

a good hard look at my life. I guess I owe you a huge thank you."

Rachel: "Thank you, for breaking up with you? What do you mean?"

Marty: "It really rattled me. Without losing something so important, I'm not sure I would've realized the change I had to make."

Rachel "Go on…" Rachael says with eyebrows lifted.

Marty: "About a month after we split, I started to see a counselor."

Rachel: "Wow, Marty, that's great. I did the same."

Marty: "You did?"

Rachel: "Yeah, you meant the world to me,"

Marty: "Likewise, so I started to make a list,"

Rachel: "A list?"

Marty: "Yeah, I started to take an inventory of everything I was grateful for, and you were at the top. And then I made a commitment to learn whatever it takes to make love every day."

Rachel: "What?! Typical. Every guy wants to have sex every day," Rachel says with an internal eye roll. *He hasn't changed a bit.*

Marty sees her body language start to close off.

Marty: "No, no, no," I realized that there's so much more to love than having sex."

Once again, Rachel's curiosity piques. He notices her attention is back, so he continues."

Marty: "What I really want to do is apologize. I truly had no idea how to love you. That being said, my ignorance is no excuse. When I say I want to make love every day, I want to hear you and understand you, I want to feel what you feel, and I want to truly allow my life to be shaped by yours. I want to hold you and let you feel so secure. I even want to pursue something that's bigger than us. When I say I want to make love every day, that's what I mean. It's been six months of therapy, and I have learned so much. My gratitude has grown, and my willingness to be taught has become my life's pursuit. But, Rachel, more than anything, I long to unlock the love *you* desire."

We will leave you with this, because we believe in you....

After decades of working with individuals and couples, we know that anyone can change. Some do overnight, and others over a lifetime. The choice is yours. Being intimate is one of the most vulnerable and rewarding experiences you can have. The fact is that you were created for this extraordinary intimate love.

~Roy and Amy

Bibliography

Amodeo, John. "What Does Intimacy Have to Do with Spirituality?" *Psychology Today.* Sussex Publishers, January 15, 2017. https://www.psychologytoday.com/us/blog/intimacy-path-toward-spirituality/201701/what-does-intimacy-have-do-spirituality.

Andersen, Charlotte Hilton. "50 Interesting Sex Facts You Probably Didn't Know." COATS COUNSELING. *Reader's Digest*, January 23, 2019. https://www.coatscounseling.com/inthemedia/50-interesting-sex-facts-you-probably-didnt-know.

Blakemore, Erin. "There Are Only Two Shakers Left in the World." Smithsonian.com. Smithsonian Institution, January 6, 2017. https://www.smithsonianmag.com/smart-news/there-are-only-two-shakers-left-world-180961701/.

Brooks, Arthur C. "Stop Waiting for Your Soul Mate." *The Atlantic.* Atlantic Media Company, April 7, 2022. https://www.theatlantic.com/family/archive/2021/09/soul-mates-love-destiny/620014/.

Brower, Naomi. "Effects of Pornography on Relationships." *Relationships Extension.* Utah State University, May 17, 2021. https://extension.usu.edu/relationships/research/effects-of-pornography-on-relationships.

Cherry, Kendra. "Why Our Brains Are Hardwired to Focus on the Negative." *Verywell Mind*, April 29, 2020. https://www.verywellmind.com/negative-bias-4589618.

Covey, Stephen R. *The Seven Habits of Highly Effective People.* New York, NY: Simon & Schuster, 1989.

Cvetkovska, Ljubica, Hermina Drah, and Nikolina Jeric. "25 Workplace Affairs Statistics for Business & Pleasure." 2Date4Love, January 28, 2022. https://2date4love.com/workplace-affairs-statistics/.

Emery, Lea Rose. "Swiping Isn't Just for Hookups." *Bustle*, March 14, 2017. https://www.bustle.com/p/how-many-people-who-meet-on-dating-apps-get-married-swiping-isnt-just-for-hookups-44359.

Escalante, Alison. "Here's How Science Says You Can Give the Perfect Hug (Once Social Distancing Is over)." *Forbes Magazine*, December 10, 2021. https://www.

BIBLIOGRAPHY

forbes.com/sites/alisonescalante/2020/06/09/how-to-give-the-perfect-hug-according-to-science/?sh=52d4b7b55f9f.

Fisher, Helen E. "Lust, Attraction, and Attachment in Mammalian Reproduction." *Human Nature* 9, no. 1 (1998): 23–52. https://doi.org/10.1007/s12110-998-1010-5.

Frost, Robert. "The Death of the Hired Man." Poetry Foundation, 1914. https://www.poetryfoundation.org/poems/44261/the-death-of-the-hired-man.

Holland, Karen J., Jerry W. Lee, Helen H. Marshak, and Leslie R. Martin. "Spiritual Intimacy, Marital Intimacy, and Physical/Psychological Well-Being: Spiritual Meaning as a Mediator." *Psychology of Religion and Spirituality* 8, no. 3 (2016): 218–27. https://doi.org/10.1037/rel0000062.

"Internet Pornography by the Numbers: A." Webroot. Accessed April 25, 2022. https://www.webroot.com/us/en/resources/tips-articles/internet-pornography-by-the-numbers.

Kessler, Sarah. "15+ Short Non-Religious Prayers for Thanks, Healing & Funerals." Cake Blog, May 27, 2021. https://www.joincake.com/blog/non-religious-prayers/.

Kubota, Taylor. "37 Sex Stats You Need to Know." *Men's Journal*. Accessed April 25, 2022. https://www.mensjournal.com/health-fitness/37-things-everyone-should-know-about-sex-20150327/.

LaMotte, Sandee. "10 Health Benefits of Having More Sex." CNN, March 12, 2018. https://www.cnn.com/2018/03/01/health/health-benefits-of-sex-parallels/index.html.

Leading Effectively Staff. "What Is Psychological Safety at Work?" Center for Creative Leadership, January 15, 2022. https://www.ccl.org/articles/leading-effectively-articles/what-is-psychological-safety-at-work/.

Lehmiller, Justin. "How Often Do Women Orgasm During Sex?" Kinsey Institute. Indiana University, January 24, 2019. https://blogs.iu.edu/kinseyinstitute/2019/01/24/how-often-do-women-orgasm-during-sex/.

Lyman, Johanna. "4 Signs You're Using Sex as a Weapon." Yahoo! GalTime.com, March 12, 2012. https://www.yahoo.com/lifestyle/tagged/health/love-sex/4-signs-youre-using-sex-weapon-144800255.html.

Members in the Media. "The Science of Prayer." Association for Psychological Science. *The Wall Street Journal*, May 20, 2020. https://www.psychologicalscience.org/news/the-science-of-prayer-2.html.

Miller, Nate. "Emotional Affairs at Work: Understanding the Limits for Close Office Relationships." *ReGain*, April 15, 2022. https://www.regain.us/advice/infidelity/emotional-affairs-at-work-understanding-the-limits-for-close-office-relationships/.

Neuman, Scott. "Fewer than Half of U.S. Adults Belong to a Religious Congregation, New Poll Shows." NPR, March 30, 2021. https://www.npr.org/2021/03/30/982671783/fewer-than-half-of-u-s-adults-belong-to-a-religious-congregation-new-poll-shows.

BIBLIOGRAPHY

Nolte, Dorothy Law. "Children Learn What They Live." *Psychology Today*. Sussex Publishers, 1972. https://www.psychologytoday.com/us/blog/overcoming-child-abuse/201112/children-learn-what-they-live.

Parrott, Les, and Leslie L. Parrott. Essay. In *Becoming Soul Mates: Cultivating Spiritual Intimacy in the Early Years of Marriage*, 164. Grand Rapids, MI: Zondervan Pub. House, 1995.

Patterson, Richard, and Joseph Price. "Pornography, Religion, and the Happiness Gap: Does Pornography Impact the Actively Religious Differently?" *Journal for the Scientific Study of Religion* 51, no. 1 (2012): 79–89. https://doi.org/10.1111/j.1468-5906.2011.01630.x.

Polanchek, Sara, and Sidney Shaw. "Ten Intimate Relationship Research Findings Every Counselor Should Know." *Counseling Today*. American Counseling Association, January 23, 2019. https://ct.counseling.org/2015/11/ten-intimate-relationship-research-findings-every-counselor-should-know/.

Prause, Nicole. "Porn Is for Masturbation." *Archives of Sexual Behavior* 48, no. 8 (November 7, 2019): 2271–77. https://doi.org/10.1007/s10508-019-1397-6.

Prochazkova, Eliska, and Mariska E. Kret. "Connecting Minds and Sharing Emotions through Mimicry: A Neurocognitive Model of Emotional Contagion." *Neuroscience & Biobehavioral Reviews* 80 (2017): 99–114. https://doi.org/10.1016/j.neubiorev.2017.05.013.

Sax, Leonard, William van Wijngaarden, Charles C. Camosy, David Cloutier, Susan Hanssen, Josh Craddock, Borys Gudziak, et al. "Living with Uncertainty." Public Discourse. The Witherspoon Institute, May 30, 2020. https://www.thepublicdiscourse.com/2020/05/64016/.

Sine, Richard. "Sex Drive: How Do Men and Women Compare?" Edited by Brunilda Nazario. WebMD, August 22, 2013. https://www.webmd.com/sex/features/sex-drive-how-do-men-women-compare.

Soukup, Ruth. "9 Conversations Every Couple Needs to Have: Healthy Marriage Tips." *Living Well Spending Less*, August 31, 2020. https://www.livingwellspendingless.com/9-conversations-spouse-need/.

"Spiritual Intimacy." Bowling Green State University. Accessed April 25, 2022. https://www.bgsu.edu/arts-and-sciences/psychology/graduate-program/clinical/the-psychology-of-spirituality-and-family/research-findings/marriage-couples/spiritual-intimacy.html.

Surendra, Aditi, and Sandip Deshpande. "Your Most Powerful Sexual Organ Is Not down There, but between Your Ears." *The News Minute*, May 27, 2021. https://www.

BIBLIOGRAPHY

thenewsminute.com/article/your-most-powerful-sexual-organ-not-down-there-between-your-ears-47541.

Thomas, Kenneth W., and Warren H. Schmidt. "A Survey of Managerial Interests with Respect to Conflict." *Academy of Management Journal* 19, no. 2 (1976): 315–18. https://doi.org/10.5465/255781.

Turner, Ash. "Texting on the Toilet, Cell Phone in Toilet Statistics 2022." *BankMyCell*, January 3, 2022. https://www.bankmycell.com/blog/cell-phone-usage-in-toilet-survey#jump1.

Vedantam, Shankar. "Researchers Explore Pornography's Effect on Long-Term Relationships." NPR, October 9, 2017. https://www.npr.org/2017/10/09/556606108/research-explores-the-effect-pornography-has-on-long-term-relationships.

"Why Bad Smells Make You Gag." Australian Broadcasting Corporation. Reuters, March 5, 2008. https://www.abc.net.au/science/articles/2008/03/05/2180489.htm.

"World Religion Day - Third Sunday in January." National Day Calendar, April 1, 2022. https://nationaldaycalendar.com/world-religion-day-third-sunday-in-january/.

"FAQs." Kinsey Institute. Indiana University. Accessed April 25, 2022. https://kinseyinstitute.org/research/faq.php.

About the Authors

Dr. Amy Clark is originally from Buffalo, New York, and now lives in Naples, Florida. After several years of leading marriage small groups at her church, she went back to school to earn her doctorate in the Ministry of Christian Counseling. Amy now partners with her husband in a private coaching and counseling practice, where they specialize in relationship and intimacy issues.

Roy served as a full-time pastor for ten years and has been coaching couples and individuals for over thirty years. He has worked with everyone from teens to retirees to help them give and experience the love they were created for. He is the author of the *Diamond King*; the founder of Mentor 1, a non-profit that finds mentors for kids; and an entrepreneur who has started several companies. His heart is to help others achieve their dreams, especially that of loving and being loved.

This is the second marriage for both Amy and Roy. They understand the heartache from relationships that feel one-sided, and they also know what it takes to have an extraordinary marriage. Their hope is to help people cultivate such a loving relationship.

Those of you who are committed to learning and practicing all four intimacies, in order, and with intentionality, are in an elite group of individuals. We welcome you to the Lovemaker Tribe and encourage you to make love, every day.

www.ingramcontent.com/pod-product-compliance
Lightning Source LLC
Chambersburg PA
CBHW070155100426
42743CB00013B/2922